Tales and Travels
of a School Inspector

Tales and Travels
of a School Inspector

John Wilson

*In the Highlands and Islands
at the end of the 19th century*

*Includes Jura, Heisker, Islay, Orkney,
Coll, Argyll, Lewis and many others*

acair

❊

This book was first published by
Jackson, Wylie & Co.
Publishers to the University,
Glasgow, in 1928.

It was printed at that time by
Robert Maclehose & Co. Ltd,
The University Press, Glasgow.

The photograph of John Wilson is reproduced with
the permission of the University of Glasgow.

Republished in 1998 and reprinted in 2006
by Acair Ltd.
7 James Street, Stornoway, Isle of Lewis.
www.acairbooks.com
info@acairbooks.com

ISBN 0 86152 143 9
9780861521432

The publishers are grateful to
Mr. Simon Fraser for bringing
this book to their attention.

THIS EDITION
Typescripted by Peigi MacLennan.
Designed by Mark Blackadder
Jacket design by Mark Blackadder
Foreword © Brian Wilson

This edition printed by ColourBooks Ltd., Dublin

❊

CONTENTS

Brian Wilson

FOREWORD

The prospect of a visit from Her Majesty's Inspectors of Schools still has the power to strike apprehension into the hearts of the most self-assured teachers and school heads. Yet in the heart of that relationship lies a respect which has been built up over many years and much experience of the Inspectorate at work. Its primary functions have not been to identify and publish failure but to report on performance and then work with fellow professionals in order to support, advise and improve.

It is easy to imagine, however, that to school teachers labouring in the furthest corners of 19th century Scotland, without the benefits of contracts or pension schemes, visits from an HMI must have seemed more than a little threatening. What conditions had the stranger endured in order to get there? What would be his mood or indeed his expectations? What might be his understanding of the social and cultural conditions under which the school operated? On such considerations their futures might depend.

That was the world which John Wilson, a native of Dufftown in Banffshire, entered as Inspector a few years after the 1872 Education Act had introduced the concept of compulsory education. His career spanned 50 years and this book was first published in 1928, shortly after his retirement. Much of his time was spent in, and most of his anecdotes stem from, the Highlands and Islands. This is what contributes greatly to the interest of his writings as a generous slice of social history.

Wilson was clearly a well-intentioned man with a profound attachment to education. He is rarely censorious in his judgements and his desire for empathy with the Gael led him into efforts to acquire a working knowledge of the language. His observations do not patronise. Yet there is the clear impression of an educated Scot constantly discovering that, in reality, there was another country within the country with its different language, traditions and social norms.

He would, during the same period, have found plenty poverty and suffering in the slums of Glasgow. But there is still a poignancy in reading his accounts of the rural destitution which occurred in many of the areas he visited. His accounts of how, for example, diseases like scarlet fever would commonly "carry off whole families" in the black-houses of Lewis, are a better guide to social conditions than any collection of statistics. It is true down to the present day – if you want to know about the economic status of any community, the condition of the children is as good a guide as any.

The Scottish education tradition, which continues to stand us in good stead as the foundation for further advances, was built around upstanding citizens like John Wilson. His book is a period piece which tells us a great deal about Scotland in general, and the Highlands and Islands in particular, during an under-reported period in their history. It is full of cameos which enhance our understanding of how people lived and, most important to John Wilson, of how they were educated. Acair have done very well to re-publish it.

BRIAN WILSON M.P.
Minister of State for Education at The Scottish Office
February 1998

John Wilson

FOREWORD

The lot of an Inspector of schools half a century ago presented many contrasts to that of his successor of to-day. The larger area with which he necessarily became familiar, the slower and more trying methods of travelling, and the widely different social and educational conditions which then obtained, entailed for him many experiences which would be impossible nowadays.

My professional career covered a period of nearly forty years. In the course of it I visited a very large number of schools of various types in half the counties of Scotland, including all the Highland ones, as well as all the Islands, with the exception of Shetland, Bute, Arran, Cumbrae and St. Kilda.

Urged by old colleagues and friends cognisant of my exceptional opportunities, I have ventured to put on record some of the incidents and impressions of a long and happy service. The selection and grouping of these has been no easy task; but it has given me one of the greatest of life's pleasures—that of recalling happy memories of the 'days of other years.'

For obvious reasons I have refrained from mentioning names of individuals and places. Autobiographical matter has been included only where it could not well be avoided.

To literary art, I need hardly add, I make no claim. My aim has been to furnish a simple record of incidental experiences, which may interest the general reader, as well as some of the many whose thoughts and activities are concerned with Scottish education.

Edinburgh, *April,* 1928.

Chapter I

INTRODUCTORY

Although I was brought up and received my early education in the parish of Keig in Aberdeenshire, I was born in the comparatively small town of Dufftown in Banffshire, important in that it was the birthplace of the distinguished soldier, Sir Donald Stuart, and Lord Mountstephen, who built the Canadian Pacific Railway across the Rockies and was created a Peer in 1891. Regarding the latter, I am constrained to record the following incident of his boyhood, when to assist his parents he was engaged to herd the cows on the farm of a distant relative of my own. The farmer's wife made her own cheese, which she stored in a small outhouse. One day she discovered that some tempting portions were missing. She had no hesitation in concluding that the little herd boy was the thief. While being duly chastised he stoutly denied the theft. Many years passed. A day came when, being now a Lord, he visited Dufftown, and was being fêted in the town hall by the inhabitants. The farmer's wife, a frail old woman, entered. His Lordship recognised her at once. Springing to his feet, he hastened towards her, and as he led her forward by the arm his first words were, "Come awa', Jean; I did steal the cheese." That lie had evidently been rankling in his mind all his life. The sight of his old mistress prompted the confession.

A schoolfellow of mine was William Benton, whose

murder in Mexico by the notorious Villa caused considerable sensation in this country.

It may interest some of my readers to know that I received part of my training in the classics in the manse of the Rev. Dr. William Pirie Smith, father of the distinguished Professor William Robertson Smith. I have occasionally sat at one side of the table while the greatest Hebraist of the day was reading a book at the other. His father, being short of stature, had to stand on a small platform in the pulpit. I have seen the beadle removing it when the father of Sir William Robertson Nicoll, late editor of the *British Weekly*, came to assist at Communions.

One afternoon I was having tea in the manse. Opposite me sat the Professor. By my side was Bertie, his youngest brother. At that time the Professor's so-called heretical opinions were causing a stir in the Free Church. During a pause in the conversation the young hopeful, who had evidently been keeping his ears open to all that was passing, suddenly broke the silence with, "I say, Willie, is it true that you don't think there's a Devil?" The Professor burst out laughing as his mother promptly tapped the interrogator's shoulder, with the remark, "Little boys must not speak when at tea."

In due course, after serving a pupil teachership, I passed through Moray House Free Church Training College and Edinburgh University, where I graduated in 1877. During my Arts course I had a number of class-fellows who rose to distinguished positions. Amongst them were Lords Sands and Salveson; the Rev. Dr. Playfair, who succeeded the Rev. Dr. Boyd of St. Andrews; the Rev. Dr. Cathels, ex-

Moderator of the Church of Scotland; and John W. Mackail, our most brilliant classical scholar.

While I am on the subject of Arts, let me record what happened at the eccentric Professor Blackie's house when a few of his best students, and particularly Gaelic-speaking ones, were invited to breakfast at eight o'clock one Saturday morning. At these functions, over which his wife, whom he declared he loved better than Pindar, presided with a quiet dignity, in marked contrast to her husband's hilarious demeanour, themes of all kinds, occasionally flavoured with Greek, came under discussion. As most of the young men had but recently quitted their beds, dreams and their interpretation naturally formed a suitable topic. One student with a lack of good taste in presence of a lady ventured to say that he had been dreaming about the parasites which find human hair their happy hunting ground. The table was convulsed with laughter, in which the Professor joined as he remarked, "And what more natural than for a fellow to dream about what's running in his head?" He was a typical 'Autocrat of the breakfast table.' Though scholarly, he never taught us much Greek. I have often wondered what he really did teach us. The most trifling incident would divert him from his function. As was his wont, he daily opened with the Lord's Prayer in Greek. One morning a disturbance in the class upset him. He paused, forgot where he was in the prayer, and asked the students to give him the last word. Almost every word was suggested. The result was a lecture on the unreliability of memory, but no Greek lesson that day.

After a brief assistantship in Wigtown Academy, I was appointed headmaster of Duffus Public School in

Morayshire. Of an evening it was always interesting to have a talk with old residenters regarding the 'ancient' history of the school, from which my two predecessors, both licentiates of the Church of Scotland, had demitted office to become in succession minister of the parish of Glenlivet. I was particularly interested in their description of cock-fighting in the old school. It reminded me of Hugh Miller's narrative in *My Schools and Schoolmasters*. It was an annual event. The bigger boys brought each a cock on the day appointed. Inside a ring of pupils, with the dominie as referee, two birds at a time fought till one or other of them succumbed to his injuries. A penny or twopence at most was the entry money. This the teacher collected, and in addition claimed the vanquished fowls. There was no Society for the Prevention of Cruelty to Animals in these days.

It was in 1882, about ten years after the passing of Lord Young's Education Act, that I joined the inspectorate. The mode of inspection then was very different from what obtains nowadays. Everything was stereotyped. Rules laid down had to be followed to the letter. The appraisement of grants, as the result of individual examination on prescribed lines according to a code to which I shall subsequently refer as the 'Cast-iron Code', lay entirely in the hands of Her Majesty' Inspector, who was often placed in a most invidious position. Luckily for him, My Lords of the Education Department almost invariably endorsed his estimate of a school. Otherwise his life would have sometimes been intolerable.

When Sir John Struthers succeeded Sir Henry Craik, 'My Lords' was dropped and 'the Department' substituted.

Thus a healthier educational atmosphere was created all round.

In the years when the Inspectors in both England and Scotland were emissaries of the Education Department the correspondence was often amusing, and did not make for confidence in the staff of the London Office. For instance, an Inspector once showed me a minute referring to a school in Skye. One official who had to deal with the matter wrote on the margin, "Where is Skye?" The colleague to whom the query was addressed wrote below, "I am not quite sure, but I think it's not far from the Orkney Islands." Before the case was settled I am confident from what the Inspector minuted that both of these officials found it advisable to revise their geography of Scotland.

When, as rarely happened, a subordinate member of the inspectorate fell short of work in his district, he was summoned to the London Office for clerical work. To this he did not object, as it afforded him an excellent opportunity of seeing the city. One man who rose to the top of the ladder told me that when he entered on duty he got through his first task so expeditiously that a deputation of the clerks approached him with a statement that if he did his work so smartly he would bring dire disaster on the whole clerical fraternity. As he was to be there only temporarily, he readily agreed to adopt their 'ca' canny' slogan. When he was leaving, one and all assured him of a warm welcome should he happen to come back. But he never did.

With these introductory remarks I shall now proceed to deal with other reminiscences, grave and gay, associated with my inspectorial career.

Chapter II

INSPECTION

IN my experience Inspectors I have met or been associated with professionally have been as varied in scholarly ability and fitness for their special work as the teachers whose labours they were appointed to criticise and appraise. Appointment to the inspectorate, in the early days at least, depended more on scholarship than teaching experience. A graduate of Oxford or Cambridge had an advantage over one possessing a Scottish University degree only. To my knowledge it oftener than once happened that a scholarly young man, who had never seen the inside of a primary school, and who had no teaching experience, was appointed to a post for which he was no more fitted than a chauffeur to be Captain of an ocean liner. Some had wisdom enough to learn their profession at the expense of the teachers. But there must have often been much heart burning in the closet over vituperative private correspondence, and perhaps merited trouncing in the public prints. But some excellent men were appointed, and proved thoroughly worthy of their high calling. It was my good fortune to be associated with more than one of these. Geniality sometimes made up for lack of inspecting ability. One man occurs to me who, though an able scholar, was very far from being an ideal examiner. He was a poet of by no means mediocre attainments, and by adopting an affable demeanour he managed to keep his light burning for many a year. I was once deputed to assist him. He sent me a characteristic letter to air his professional difficulties and at the same time thank me for my assistance. The P.S. he added ran thus:

> Bairns to left of him;
> Bairns to right of him;
> Bairns quite in spite of them,
> stumbled and blundered —
> I'd rather be lammin' them — Still I'll examine them —
> But *not* the six hundred — (at least in a week).

While working for him I sometimes found his eccentricity rather irritating, as when he sent me a letter fixing the school I was to examine on a particular day. He added a P.S. as follows: "Don't forget the busy bee." Over this injunction I lost a whole night's sleep. To associate a school examination with a member of an apiary fairly puzzled me. However, it somewhat allayed my anxiety to reflect that a school might by a stretch of imagination be considered by a man of this type a hive of industry. Accordingly, I concluded his reference must be to it as a unit. When I reached the school I soon solved the riddle. I found that the female assistant's parchment certificate was then due, as her second year's probation, indicated by B on the schedule, established. The lady, I was pleased to find, was a very proficient busy bee, and I certainly did not forget her.

The first Inspector under whom I worked was a brilliant graduate of Oxford, a capable examiner, and a man

who always enjoyed a good joke. It was in an Inverness
school that I happened to be examining a class in botany.
Having set the pupils to write answers to a few questions I
had written on a blackboard, I was engrossed in other work
when the Inspector, who made no pretensions to a
knowledge of plant life, crossed the room. He naturally
paused to glance at the questions. As he passed out, the
pupils, with all eyes on the board, burst into loud laughter.
The cause was obvious. He had changed the question,
"What is the difference between a corm and a bulb?" into
"What is the difference between a *corn* and a *bunion?*"

His face was a study when a small boy corrected him
one day. He was seated in a chair with a class of infants in
front of him. The school was old, and the well-worn floor
was full of small holes. From one of these there emerged a
small animal, which fearlessly began to nibble at some
crumbs. The Inspector, struck with the absence of shyness,
naturally attributed this to the good feeling existing
between the children and the lower animals. In the course
of his comments he made frequent use of the word 'mouse,'
till an urchin at his elbow whispered in a confidential tone,
"Please, sir, it's nae a mouse, it's a young rattie." This information, which was correct, convinced the Inspector that his
knowledge of zoology was in need of overhauling.

One day I accompanied a genial Inspector to a school
in Banffshire. In the railway compartment seated beside
him was a gentleman of his acquaintance, with whom he
entered into conversation. The Inspector evinced much
interest in his friend's son, whom he had examined as a boy.
On his being informed that the lad was then at Mergui, he,

apparently ignorant of its geographical position, asked where it was situated. Subsequently, I heard him examining the highest class in geography. One of his questions was, "Where is Mergui?" Getting no reply, he turned to the teacher and, drawing a serious face, said, "Oh, it's fair ridiculous that the pupils don't know where a well-known place like that is." I could have told a tale *in* school; but I didn't. I knew quite well the incident would not adversely affect the Inspector's estimate of the class's geographical knowledge.

This same Inspector one day made the discovery that his tests in arithmetic were being passed on from one school to another. It came about in this way. In a certain school, after he had supplied each pupil with a test card, a boy jumped up, and to the intense discomfiture of his teacher shouted, "Please, sir, I did these sums yesterday." The result was that the Inspector handed out a new set of cards. It is not recorded, but doubtless before the day was over that indiscreet youngster got what he would remember till the end of his natural life.

I can recall a very amusing experience I had in a Lewis school taught with moderate success by a well-developed, red-haired Highland Hebe. I was examining a class of bad readers arranged along a wall facing me. Glancing over my shoulder, the teacher noted that I was putting more cyphers, indicating failures, on the form than she considered justifiable. Her patience exhausted, she in a wrathful tone exclaimed, "Look here, Mr. Wilson, if you fail my children like that, I'll take the life of you." A glance at her face satisfied me that she was prepared to go to any extreme in the shape of assault, and I am bound to admit that for the nonce casting aside My Lords' injunctions as to passes and failures, I treated the remainder of the class with a leniency which soothed her wounded feelings, and enabled me to enjoy in her parlour the excellent lunch to which she invited me at the conclusion of the examination.

It once fell to my lot to have to conduct an examination barefooted. The school was situated in a very remote part of a mountainous island of the Inner Hebrides. To reach it I had to leave the main road and make my way as best I could by a sort of track across waste moorland, rough boulders and streams, the largest of which had to be negotiated by stepping-stones. For more than a mile it was a hop, step, and leap mode of progression. Here I may mention that on the occasion of my first visit to this school I had to run the gauntlet of a number of ferocious mongrel dogs as I passed some crofters' houses. Before leaving the inn I armed myself with a good cudgel, kindly lent by the innkeeper, who fore-warned me of the risk of being bitten. To make safety almost certain I arranged for a schoolboy, who was on good terms with the canine fraternity of the district, to meet me at the edge of the danger zone. Thus escorted, I managed to reach the school without trouble.

But let me revert to my barefooted experience. The day happened to be unusually wet and stormy, with all the streams in full flood. However, this did not deter me. I braved the elements, with the inevitable result that when I reached the school I was literally soaked from head to foot. Luckily there was a good fire of peats glowing in the grate. Dreading the consequences of wet feet in a district where medical attendance was at a low ebb, I unhesitatingly doffed my wet shoes and stockings, emptied the water out of the former and wrung the latter, which I suspended from a string before the fire to dry against the completion of the examination, to which I then addressed myself. That the Inspector was barefooted seemed not in the least to amuse the pupils, almost all of whom were without shoes and stockings. The inspection being concluded and the school dismissed, I drew a chair to the fire, and was in the act of wiping my feet with the blackboard duster, when I discovered that the fender on which they rested had been unstintingly blackleaded on the previous evening, thus rendering the soles as black as a negro's. However, I managed with what water was still on the floor in some degree to remove the objectionable pigment, and not a moment too soon, for the teacher's wife entered the room as I was tying the last shoe knot.

It was in Strathconon in Ross-shire that I examined a boy in a unique situation. He was the son of a shepherd, and was prevented from attending the annual examination on account of an injury to his leg. The teacher explained the case, adding that he was a most promising pupil and very fond of the school. It was reported that he had been crying all night because he was unable to be present along with his class-fellows. The zeal of the youngster touched me. It was not every day that so much juvenile enthusiasm in learning was met with. Accordingly, on my homeward journey I halted at the father's cottage, which happened to be near the turnpike. I entered, examined and 'passed' the patient in his bed, much to the delight of the parents, and particularly of the zealous examinee. By this act I gathered that my reputation as a kindly man was considerably enhanced in the strath.

The following is another case in which I had to examine a pupil in a farmer's cart. I was just leaving the island of Jura after having completed the inspection of the schools. A girl twelve years of age, daughter of a gamekeeper, who lived fully twelve miles from the nearest school and had to be taught at home, failed on account of stormy weather to turn up for examination at the annual visit of the Inspector. In a case of this kind the managers generally provided a conveyance if the parent did not possess one. I had completed about half my journey to the ferry where I was to cross to Islay, when far off across the heathery moorland I descried a conveyance of some sort coming in my direction. In due time a cart appeared, in which, amongst abundance of straw, were seated the absentee with her girl teacher. The father, who was in charge, expressed surprise when he saw me. Hoping that I was still in the inn, and being desirous to have his daughter examined, he had risked the long journey. What was I to do? Happy thought! Telling my driver to go ahead at walking pace, I bade the father turn his cart and follow, so that no time might be lost. I then got into the cart, and as we jolted along over the moor I applied the usual tests, even to arithmetic on a slate, and satisfied myself that the girl was being well taught for her age and circumstances. The task finished, with a few words of praise, followed by the father's "Well, sir, I am sure you never examined a pupil in a cart before," I re-entered my own conveyance and hastened to the ferry. It was certainly an odd experience; but I had a feeling of satisfaction in having done a kindly thing, which I am sure brought relief to at least one anxious mind.

Away up behind Fort William is situated the small school of Blarmacfoldach, efficiently taught in my time by a self-possessed Highland lady. The annual inspection took place in December, in which month there was sometimes considerable difficulty in reaching this outlying seminary. The winter when what I am about to relate took place had been very severe, and my undertaking to visit the school was at the risk of being smothered in snow before I reached it. Officers of the Education Department, like the men of Nelson's navy, were expected to do their duty, and I, being young and fairly athletic, had no desire to shirk mine, even though I had little hope in such inclement weather of finding a single pupil present. For a mile or two I managed to get along without mishap in a sleigh drawn by two heavy horses. After that the wreaths of snow became so deep and numerous that the road, or rather track, was obliterated. I now found it necessary to abandon the sleigh and wade up through the heather on the mountain side, till I found the snow less deep. At this elevation I proceeded in the direction of the school, which I reached after infinite exertion and no end of falls. The roof only was visible till I was quite near it. The door was in the gable, and about a yard in front of it was a wreath about ten feet high, on the brink of which I at last found myself. Losing my balance, I slid down its slope, and, bursting open the door, came sprawling into the schoolroom on all fours in a smother of snow. I often wonder if ever an Inspector entered a school in such an undignified manner. Wonderful to relate, all the twenty pupils were present, and it need hardly be said the teacher was only too glad to see me. Seeing no conveyance, she had begun to fear that the inspection of her school would be put off indefinitely. As I sat at her desk, water was drip, dripping in front of me from the ceiling. This she explained was due to snow melting on the roof. It was coming through her living-room in the storey above, and thence into the schoolroom. Teachers in remote corners in those days had often to tolerate grievances of this sort. But a surprise was awaiting me. At the conclusion of the examination the pupils were dismissed, while I spent a few minutes inspecting the necessary forms and registers. When I came out and looked around not a single child was to be seen, nothing but a dreary waste of snow. "Where have they all gone?" I asked the teacher. The incident of the disappearing band in Scott's *Lady of the Lake* occurred to me. "Oh," she replied, "they have just gone home the way they came here." Now when drifting snow is blowing towards a wall, or in this case a dry stone dyke, an open space often occurs between the two no matter how high the wreath may be. Into this channel or tunnel-like passage, where there was plenty of shelter, the pupils had glided, and scurried along like rats in the direction of their respective homes. This explained how rapidly they disappeared immediately they left the school.

From the nature of his profession it is natural to expect that an Inspector of long experience becomes known to a wide range of humanity. This sometimes has its advantages. I happened to leave my bag containing official papers in a tramway car in Glasgow. By a device I contrived to overtake it in a crowded thoroughfare. I was much relieved when the conductor smilingly handed me the bag as he remarked, "A girl found it below your seat, and as she left the car gave it to me, saying that it belonged to Mr. Wilson, a School Inspector." I regretted that I had not an opportunity of rewarding that observant damsel.

Again, I was one day walking leisurely along Oxford Street in London, when some one approaching me from behind said, "It's a nice day, Mr. Wilson," and passed on without further remark. Gazing after him, I was horrified to see a young man in shabby clothes and dilapidated shoes. He had evidently fallen on evil days, recognised me as his old Inspector, and found the temptation to address me in passing irresistible.

I have heard it said that the earliest race of Inspectors sometime took their work less seriously than their successors. I was told of one well-known Lowland Inspector who had a penchant for snuff. When inspecting a certain school, doubtless to enliven the proceedings, he asked the boys of a class in front of him where snuff, or, as he called it, 'Taddy,' could be procured. Of course every boy knew that, just as every boy in the slums of a city knows the situation of a pawnshop. I am not imagining this. I have proved it over and over again. I have even found pupils proud and anxious to enlighten me, as if they were conveying information which at some time or other I might find useful. But as to the 'Taddy,' every boy in the class volunteered to go for it. One was selected, and on his returning with a goodly-sized packet the Inspector for a joke, anxious to see the effect, passed it round the class, at the same time inviting each boy to partake of the unusual luxury. Boys will be boys. They were delighted. With much suppressed laughter one and all took a liberal pinch. The result can easily be imagined. The sneezing was terrific. The discipline of the whole school was upset. The teacher trembled at the prospect of losing the grant for the good behaviour of his pupils, and yet it was the Inspector who was primarily at fault. Had he withheld the discipline grant there would have been trouble in store for him. A complaint would have been forwarded to the Department, when doubtless My Lords would have visited this patent indiscretion of their emissary with well-merited censure. But the incident, like others of a similar nature, belongs to a bygone age. *Tempora mutantur et nos mutamur in illis.*

While some Inspectors were not devoid of humour, I knew more than one possessed of deep human sympathy, in sharp contrast to those who might be inclined to be captious and unsympathetic. I shall never forget an incident in the life of a very popular Inspector, whose sphere of labour lay for many years in the North of Scotland. A young female teacher of a small school had been seduced by a local farmer under a promise of marriage, which he refused to implement. Of course she lost her situation, and failed to get employment to enable her to support herself and child, which died shortly after it was born. Wherever she went the curse was on her. Ultimately, she drifted southwards to Glasgow in the hope of getting suitable occupation, where her past history would be unknown. Having learned her lesson, she struggled to lead a chaste life; but an evil fate seemed to be her familiar. One cold winter night, in the neighbourhood of the Clyde, this Inspector, who possessed a marvellous memory for faces, an inestimable gift, recognised her in a state of abject destitution. He at once stopped and spoke to her. He remembered the lassie he was wont to compliment for her successful teaching. Her sad tale touched him to the core. The result was that he took her to his own home, where she became governess to his young family. Everything considered, a more Christian act savouring of the good Samaritan could hardly be conceived. The poor girl, homeless and friendless in a great city, was through his instrumentality saved from a life of misery, or, what is more likely, a nameless grave. Truly, this Inspector was a man among men. I knew him well. He was one of my best friends.

Chapter III

A WIDENING CURRICULUM

To test the proficiency of children in the three R's, the abbreviation for reading, writing and arithmetic, was always an easy matter, especially if the examiner had been a teacher himself. When, however, new subjects were introduced into the curriculum the case was sometimes different. It was in an Alloa evening school that I was first called upon to examine a class of young lads in shorthand. With Pitman I had absolutely no acquaintance. I could not even follow the example of the teacher who undertook to teach a pupil Spanish, and succeeded admirably by keeping one lesson ahead of him. The class was taught by a master who had made the subject a hobby. I knew this, and it did not add to my peace of mind. However, I carefully planned my procedure beforehand. When the list of examinees was produced I opened the proceedings with a business air, but in reality the *aequus animus* was sadly wanting. Two blackboards being produced, I selected a smart-looking pupil, and, bringing him behind one of them out of sight of the class, I bade him write in shorthand a few simple sentences, which I handed him on a slip of paper. When he did this I dismissed him, and, bringing forward another pupil, requested him to write in longhand what his class-fellow had just written in shorthand. By this ding-dong method I was hopeful of overtaking my task, and at the same time camouflaging my ignorance of the subject. The effort of the second lad far from tallied with my sentences. The teacher, who had been quietly taking stock of my method of examination, now broke in. He explained that the shorthand writing was incorrect, and that as a consequence the second pupil had made a mess of his part of the test. I could not help seeing the force of his argument. With some excuse as to my being overworked, which was in a sense quite true, I finished up by requesting him to test the pupils himself, at the same time impressing upon him my reliance on his sense of fairness. Next year I was able to examine his class myself.

Almost up to the beginning of this century drawing in primary schools was optional. When professed it was examined by retired officers of the Royal Engineers appointed by the then Science and Art Department. These men, armed with packets of drawing cards for the different standards, went from school to school. But a day came when this branch was taken over by the Education Department. To the ordinary district Inspectors was entrusted the examination of the primary schools. While I was in entire agreement with the universal teaching of drawing, I could not help thinking that in certain circumstances the time devoted to it might be more profitably employed. This was forcibly brought home to me when examining a school in a mining district of Stirlingshire. As the girls of a senior class were busy struggling with the outlines of a teapot, the spout of which was missing, I strolled behind them, when I noticed that one big girl of fourteen years, on the verge of leaving school, had holes the size of half-crowns in the heels of her stockings. It at once occurred to me that she would have been more usefully employed learning to darn than trying to outline a defective teapot, a task which to her would be of no practical value in after life, when she went out to domestic service, and might ultimately become the mother of a working miner's children.

One winter I visited an evening school in a rural district of Perthshire where drawing was being taught to a class of about a score of farmers' sons and farm servants. Aiming at prescribing as a test a subject with which all were sure to be familiar, I selected a 'horse.' To draw a horse at any time is difficult, but I wished to see what success would attend their efforts. Of course, the drawing had to be done from memory. When I gave out the task, for what reason let the psychologist explain, the lads burst out laughing. However, noting that I was in earnest, they all buckled to in silence. The results were ludicrous in the extreme. It may seem incredible, but some intelligent-looking lads accustomed to handle horses daily actually reversed the position of the knees in both fore and hind legs. One or two even put both eyes on one side of the head profile. They all laughed heartily at their own drawings. They saw that something was wrong; yet they failed, when questioned, to point out the inaccuracy.

The criticism of singing was to be avoided by the Inspector who had no ear for music. It was an optional subject, but almost every school professed it. To secure the special grant a list of twelve songs, which the pupils had been taught to sing, was presented to the Inspector at his annual visit. From this he selected one or more according to the time at his disposal. One Inspector, who was as devoid of an ear for music as a scarecrow, was frequently imposed upon. When he left the district his successor, who was a keen musician, visited the school of a teacher who used to boast of his method of hoodwinking the Inspector. At his first visit the 'new broom' chose a song from the list submitted. To his surprise the words were not sung to the orthodox air. Instead of drawing the teacher's attention to this, he selected another and still another, only to find that nearly half the songs were sung to the same air as the first one. It was a case of sheer laziness to teach singing. But the teacher had practised the deception too long. He probably lost a night's sleep over his being found out. He certainly lost the grant for Singing.

One teacher half a century ago, who was not in love with the terpsichorean art, sent his Inspector the following letter:

Dear Sir,
I have come to the conclusion that singing in school is a misappropriation of much valuable time, and I have resolved to give it up. If you think I am taking a wrong course I will esteem it a great favour if you will kindly tell me so—*in confidence* of course, etc.

I am quite certain the Inspector, who was fully appreciative of the influence of singing as an item in school routine, did not see eye to eye with the writer, and would insist on its being taught.

I almost invariably selected the Gaelic song from the list in a Highland school. But in doing so I once made a mistake in a small school in Strathglass. The pupils had hardly begun to sing the song when I discovered that it consisted of something like twenty verses. If the whole lot were sung I was almost certain to have missed my train. Accordingly, I accepted a sample, and pleased the teacher by expressing my appreciation of the singing as well as the sentiments which the song conveyed.

Needlework, and in the evening schools dressmaking and millinery, had to receive attention from the district Inspector. The young Oxford graduate, greatly daring, sometimes felt that in justification of his high calling he was bound to make some pretence to a knowledge of the *seams* — the generic term applied to all forms of needlework. I heard of one who in a moment of officiousness made this comment on the garment in hand: "That's not like the way my wife's garments are made." To this the very capable instructress replied: "I dinna ken what your wife wears next her skin, but I ken them chemises are a' richt."

It is now many years since needlework had to be taught in primary schools according to an official schedule. When this new arrangement was launched the local dressmakers, who taught sewing in remote Highland schools, took fright at the sight of a detailed printed list of requirements. As a rule they were the only instructresses available, and, to their credit be it said, they generally did their work passing well. Some of them threatened to give up teaching. To obviate this, knowing that they were quite capable of carrying out all that the schedule demanded, I got an expert teacher of needlework to make up specimens of what was required for each class. These I got nicely arranged in the form of a handy book, which I carried with me on my daily rounds to show to the teachers who had expressed hesitancy to undertake the work. At this moment I can see how eagerly the old bodies scanned these specimens. On my asking if their girls could do similar ones, the invariable reply was, "Oh, yes, they could easily do these," and they did. The terror inspired by a printed sheet had passed away. The poor seamstresses once more breathed freely.

Specialist teachers of needlework were as a rule proud of their girls' work. I always thought it a regrettable omission on the part of the Inspector should he leave the school without examining what had been accomplished with so much patient labour. It was in a Forfarshire school that on the completion of the ordinary work I strolled into a room where the needlework was carefully laid out for inspection. A finer display of sewing and knitting I had seldom set eyes on. I made a thorough examination of the work, and heartily praised its excellence. But imagine my surprise when I was told that I was the first Inspector who had looked at the sewing in more than a dozen years. Hearing this, I reflected that the district Inspector might have considered it *infra dig* to handle female underwear. In explanation of the omission I advanced my opinion that the Inspector was doubtless aware of the excellence of the teaching, and consequently did not trouble to examine the garments. The lady smiled and simply muttered "Possibly." But I felt quite certain she knew that I was only trying to explain away the neglect or indifference of a colleague.

One evening I was visiting classes for young women who were undergoing a course of physical training in a town's school. One of the instructresses was a certificated teacher of a class in the day school. Being fond of it, she took up this form of evening work as a hobby. She was well qualified, and produced results quite as good as those who specialised in physical drill. When she had finished and was about to depart, I said to her, "Now Miss —, since you are so fond of this work and so successful, why don't you go in for it in preference to ordinary primary school teaching?" Drawing herself up with a pout on her lips, she replied, "Do you think I would care to climb these ropes and ladders when I come to fifty years of age?" The possibility of her having to do so had never occurred to me. To this point I had always associated this branch with young instructresses. But undoubtedly a day was bound to come when the energy of youth would have passed away and irksomeness would take the place of what once afforded the greatest pleasure.

The foregoing subjects selected from the school curriculum are intended to divert the reader rather than to emphasise their importance in the daily routine of school work.

Chapter IV

TRAVELLING
BY LAND

When I joined the inspectorate travelling was often fraught with many anxieties and inconveniences. Luckily, toll gates across the highways had almost disappeared. To an Inspector hurrying to catch a train they were something of a nuisance. One man told me he was driving in a dogcart to the nearest railway station, and had not a minute to spare. The toll woman was old and provokingly slow. However, the cumbrous gate being opened and the fee paid, the driver whipped up his horse, when the woman was heard bawling loudly after him. Thinking of the possibility of an error in the payment, the Inspector bade him turn back. One can imagine his chagrin when the woman said, "I just wanted to tell ye that gin ye had come this gaet the morn ye wudna hae had to pay ony toll." This meant that the gate was to be removed that night. For this valuable piece of information I am quite certain the Inspector's inmost thoughts would not bear recording.

One of my most trying railway journeys was between Dalwhinnie and Inverness. It was in the middle of a severe winter. Two of us had been inspecting schools in the Fort William district. The usual way of returning to headquarters was by mail gig or a hired conveyance from Fort William to Dalwhinnie, and thence by train to Inverness. From an old time-table which we consulted we gathered that a train for Inverness left Dalwhinnie at 7 p.m., a late enough hour on a winter night. To catch it we left Fort William at 1 p.m. in a carriage and pair for the fifty miles' drive. Arriving at the station, we were horrified to be informed by the stationmaster that there was no passenger train till the forenoon of the following day, which was Sunday. But he added that we could travel by a goods train about due provided we paid first-class fare and did the journey at our own risk. This was grateful and comforting news. However, as there was no hotel available, and we were both anxious to be home, we decided to pay and trust in Providence for a safe journey. A more disagreeable one could hardly be imagined after such a long cold drive across a snow-covered country. In the guard's van in which we travelled was a tiny stove that emitted more noxious fumes than heat. The guard, who was a model of civility, did his utmost to make us comfortable amongst piles of miscellaneous goods. Reading was impossible, even had one desired to do so to pass the time, for the small railwayman's lamp shed only a flickering light sufficient to enable us to grasp our surroundings. The eternal jolting, the long halts at every station for shunting purposes, with concomitant bumping, combined to banish sleep. After much suffering we reached our destination in the small hours of Sunday morning without mishap. It was our first and last experience of the kind.

Perhaps one of the most dangerous and awe-inspiring

roads in my experience was that between Applecross and Kishorn in the west of Ross-shire. Of necessity, I took advantage of the mail dogcart in crossing the Bealach between the two places. On this mountain the road at its highest point rises to 2000 feet above sea-level. To arrange for my crossing on the following day I interviewed the postman, a weather-beaten, wiry, middle-aged man, who was only too pleased to have me for a passenger. The fact that one of the iron wheel rings of his 'ramshackle' conveyance was wobbling and in a loose condition was not difficult of explanation when I beheld the hazardous nature of the road he had to traverse on his daily round. From Applecross it rose steadily till the summit was reached. Then the descent on the Kishorn side became appallingly steep, with numerous zig-zags and hairpin bends, such as would test the most skilful motor-cycle driver in Great Britain. Owing to the steepness the narrow track was very rough and weather-worn. But I shall never forget the profusion of exquisite parsley ferns which covered a retaining wall towards the foot of the eastern side. The contemplation of these distracted my mind from the thoughts of possible accident in such a perilous situation.

From the top of Bealach the panoramic view was simply entrancing and could never be effaced from the memory. Away inland stretched innumerable bens and heathery slopes, weird and gloomy. To the west one could see the Skye mountains. My chief regret, from an artist's point of view, was at not beholding a sunset from such an elevation. From the driver's description, and I have no reason to doubt him, it must be seen to be believed.

Few horses will pass a wheel-barrow, a perambulator, or a bag of peats by the roadside without shying. Drivers knew this and kept a strict rein when nearing such objects. Strange to say, the same precaution had to be observed when approaching two women walking side by side. One was almost sure to leave her companion and cross the road in front of the horse. Let those who can explain this. An old saying was current in those days, "Beware of a cow, a sow, and a woman." Each of these had time and again been proved guilty of the indiscretion of crossing the road on the approach of a horse-drawn vehicle.

One Saturday I was returning from the inspection of Earbusaig School in Ross-shire. The hotelkeeper of Plockton was driving the small dogcart in which we were seated, with the teacher of the school between us. We were thus three abreast. The road was narrow. At a point where danger was greatest, unfortunately, some thoughtless person had left a goodly sized sack of peats by the roadside. The pony, a small skittish animal, seeing it, at once sprang to one side. A wheel hit the wall, and in the twinkling of an eye we were all three sprawling on the bank, the teacher on top of me, and some yards ahead a big leg of mutton which the hotel-keeper had wisely purchased for my Sunday dinner as he whiled away the time waiting for me till the conclusion of the examination. But the pony—oh, where was he? Off, galloping like the wind with what remained of the harness dangling at his heels. Luckily, my injuries were mostly superficial. Lying up over Sunday, I was fit to resume my official duties on Monday in a phaeton kindly lent by the local Free Church minister.

Conveyances were not always to be had, particularly in the tourist season. As showing the straits to which one was sometimes reduced, I may mention that I had once to make the journey from the school to the hotel in which I was staying in the local hearse. The natives of at least one village through which I passed appeared to be immensely amused at the sight of the Inspector on the box seat beside the driver.

When I visited the island of Coll some years ago the Commissioners connected with small holdings had pre-arranged for the sole use of the only conveyance belonging to the hotel. To meet my difficulty the local factor kindly offered me his gig, provided I took charge of the horse myself, as his man was too much engaged in agricultural work to be at my service. Needless to say, I readily accepted his offer when visiting the schools; but I must admit it took some weeks before the aroma of the byres and other unsavoury places, in which I had to stable and unharness the horse, left me.

I have oftener than once had to ride on horseback to a school. It was during the tourist season of 1884 that I failed to get a conveyance of any kind to take me from Arisaig Hotel, where I was then sojourning, to Polnish School. But the worthy priest of this Roman Catholic district kindly came to my aid. Hearing of my plight, he said I could have the use of his horse, if I cared to ride. Being quite familiar with horses when in my teens, I was grateful for his offer. Now it happened that at one point in a wood the road took what might be described as a hairpin bend up one side of a stream and down the other. When traversing this loop it occurred to me that one on horseback could easily ride through the trees, cross the stream, and regain the road on the other side, thus saving a journey of fully half-a-mile. Accordingly, on returning from the school I took this short cut through the trees and bushes. But hear the sequel. When I was in Arisaig next year the good father, in course of conversation, mentioned that I must have taken his horse through the trees when I visited Polnish School. Not denying it, I solicited an explanation. He narrated that shortly after I had been there he had gone one dark, stormy night to administer extreme unction to a dying woman in the Polnish neighbourhood. On his return journey, when he entered the wood the darkness was so intense that he failed to distinguish the road. In the circumstances there was nothing for it but to let the horse find the way. After a time he was suddenly alarmed to find branches hitting him on the face. The fate of Absalom flashed across his mind. But Providence, as he said, befriended him, and he came scatheless through an ordeal which might quite well have had a disastrous ending.

It is acknowledged that horses have wonderful memories. This one was no exception. He remembered the short cut and took it. I shudder to think what my feelings would have been had my indiscretion resulted in a vacancy in the priesthood.

Let me record an incident which happened in Moidart, a region teeming with tales of Prince Charlie. The district Inspector and I sailed from Arisaig to inspect Glenuig School. Unfortunately, we reached the school fully an hour behind the appointed time through our yacht being badly becalmed. Mrs. Blackburn, the distinguished bird painter, and wife of the professor who owned Roshven, was waiting for us. She at once soundly rated the Inspector for his unpunctuality. Knowing that it was useless to argue with her, he waited *aequo animo* till she had exhausted her vituperative eloquence before quietly asking, "Do you think I could make the wind?" Blushing, she neither affirmed nor denied the possibility of his usurping the function of Aeolus. Having had her say, she grew calm. The inspection concluded, she shook hands warmly with both of us, at the same time expressing her pleasure at having been present at the examination.

Our yacht had meantime returned to Arisaig. Unfortunately, after we had partaken of a sumptuous lunch, consisting of typical Highland fare, at the board of the hospitable laird of Glenuig, the weather became so gloomy and threatening that he tried to dissuade us from attempting to proceed on foot the nine miles to Kinlochailort hotel. He was the more insistent on our staying in his house because most of the way was then a mere bridle path leading through woods and broken up with endless ruts and holes, which made walking even in daylight somewhat dangerous. But the Inspector had friends expecting him in Arisaig. As they would naturally be alarmed should he fail to turn up, he was determined to essay the journey at all hazards. Of course, being younger than he, not to mention my being his subordinate, I was quite agreeable to accompany him. We took leave of our good friend and started off. For miles the path was so obscured by trees that we had to proceed in Indian file, I leading, with a white handkerchief held behind my back for the guidance of my companion, whose eyesight was not of the best. We had gone about four miles, when, obsessed with the roughness of the track and the gathering darkness, I happened to remark that an accident to one's limbs on such a road with no wayside house near would be a sad misfortune. The words were barely uttered when, as bad luck would have it, my foot went into a deep rut, with the result that my right ankle was badly sprained. The pain was almost unbearable, but nothing could be done to allay it. Suffice it to say I had to cover the remaining five miles limping along as I leaned heavily on my companion's arm. I was in torture all the time. It was past midnight when we reached the hotel. Luckily the conveyance from Arisaig that had been arranged for had not returned home. The sleepy driver was roused and the horses yoked. Completely worn out, we were both glad, and our friends relieved, when we arrived at Arisaig Hotel in the small hours of the morning.

To visit Ardlussa School at the north end of the island of Jura the Inspector had almost always to undergo a certain amount of inconvenience, if not of risk. In the beginning of this century he had to drive to Laag, a farm nine miles from the inn at Small Isles. Here the farmer, a retired teacher, kindly supplied a boat to take him the remaining seven miles by sea. In course of time, however, a passable road was constructed between Laag and Ardlussa, thus obviating the necessity of the sea portion of the journey. This enabled the Inspector to drive all the eighteen miles in the hotel dogcart, drawn by a horse which, excellent though he was in some respects, was more suited for ploughing than trotting.

On the occasion to which I am to refer the day was exceptionally cold and stormy. A north wind was blowing so fiercely that the head keeper of Ardlussa, at whose house the Inspector always partook of much hospitality, tried to dissuade me from attempting the return journey to Small Isles. Being a keen deer-stalker, he knew all the risks begotten of inclement weather in these regions. "If you go," said he "you will be blown over the rocks." But my driver, the innkeeper, a native of the island, was anxious to be home; nor was I averse to run considerable risks, so we set out. As may be imagined, we passed a most trying time, with more than one hairbreadth escape from the predicted disaster. When at last we reached the inn I was so cold and benumbed that I could with the greatest difficulty descend from the conveyance. Though heavily clad, I shivered from head to foot. Entering the inn, a temperance one, I luckily met the excise officer who had charge of the bonded warehouses in the adjoining distillery. My wretched appearance appealed to him. "You would be the better of a glass of whisky," said he. "A glass," I echoed. "A couple of glasses would suit me better." On this he invited me across to his office, where he had a variety of samples. To one of these, I admit, I did ample justice. A warm glow crept over me as I betook myself to the inn, where I appeased my hunger with tea accompanied by the finest of homecured ham and eggs. After that I felt fit to return to Ardlussa had such a step been necessary.

One of my most disagreeable experiences occurred one winter in Argyll. The Great War had just come to an end. The hotels, where soldiers had been quartered, were being vacated. They were sometimes left in such an unsatisfactory condition that it took weeks before they were ready to meet public requirements.

I had just finished the examination of Strontian School on Loch Sunart. Being assured that I could find accommodation in the hotel at Ardgour, about fourteen miles distant, and in the neighbourhood of a school I intended to inspect on the following day, I ventured in very stormy weather to make the journey. It was beginning to get dark, and snowing pretty heavily, with a snell wind blowing, by the time I reached Ardgour. Imagine my feelings when the hotel-keeper's wife met me, shivering with cold, with the statement that accommodation for even one night, all I asked, was impossible, since the soldiers, who had been quartered there to guard the Caledonian Canal, had left the rooms in a very disordered and unsavoury condition. She had not found time to improve matters, as her husband was lying ill with influenza, and she had no maidservant. Here was a nice fix. What was I to do? After pondering for a little I made up my mind to try the postmistress, who had a house and post-office combined about half-a-mile along the seashore. When I struggled her length, in the face of driving snow, I was chagrined to be informed that she could not find it convenient to give me a bedroom. The next house, some distance further along, was the manse of the Established Church minister. Though I did not know him, I had heard of his kindly and hospitable nature, so in desperation I risked inflicting myself upon him and his good lady. By the time I reached the manse I was completely exhausted, habited as I was in a big travelling ulster. I interviewed him in the drawing-room, into which I had been ushered with much courtesy by his wife. On my explaining my plight he expressed his sincere regret that every bed in the manse was in use, as two relatives had just arrived on the previous day. At the same time, being resolved to do what he could for me, he suggested that I might get accommodation in a lone house up on the hill-side occupied by a widow and her daughter. He added that she sometimes had sawmillers boarded with her, but that one of them was reported to have left the district. By this time I was feeling fit to sleep in a cowshed, if even that had been available. However, I was a trifle relieved when he kindly offered to guide me by the nearest path to the widow's door. We trudged up the hill-side through long grass and heather, over which the keen wind was blowing the drifting snow. He knocked on the door, and the widow appeared. But, alas! when my predicament was explained, she said she was sorry that she could not take me in, because the storm of the previous night had smashed the roof-light of the garret in which was the only bed available. She also added that the place was consequently full of snow. To confirm her statement she requested us to take a few steps backwards, when we could see the broken roof-light for ourselves. This we did, and realised that what she said was only too true. However, *necessitas non habet legem,* so I returned to the 'attack.' Now it happened that her daughter was the teacher of the small side school at Conaglen, which I had made up my mind to visit next day. On my acquainting her of my intention, the good woman, no doubt reflecting that anything she could do for me in such circumstances would likely be to her girl's advantage, suggested that if a humble shake-down in the parlour would satisfy me she would only be too pleased to make me as comfortable as circumstances would permit. To this I readily agreed. Thanking his Reverence for the trouble I had given him, I hurried off to retrieve my bag, which I had left at the hotel. When I returned it cheered me to find a glowing fire of peats in the room apartment of the but-and-ben cottage and the table laid for tea. On newly baked scones and fresh eggs I made a hearty meal, for I was both fatigued and hungry, having tasted no food since I left Strontian.

About ten o'clock the widow and her daughter, a bonnie Highland lass in her teens, whom I had not seen before, entered the apartment laden with bedding materials. Under my supervision they arranged the shake-down on the floor to my satisfaction. The storm without was still raging when I peeped out before laying me down for the night. I must have slept soundly, for daylight was creeping in at the small window before I awoke. As I lay for some moments thinking of my unique experience and the trials that sometimes beset the Inspector, whose couch at least is not always the proverbial bed of roses, my eyes lighted on what I at first concluded was my white shirt lying at my feet. But I reflected that this was hardly possible. I got up to investigate, when, lo! I discovered that it was not snow-white linen, but actual snow, which, whizzing in at the foot of the door all through the night, had formed a small wreath against the clothes at my feet. However, I had suffered no bad effects, but I shall always have a keen recollection of the wintry night when I had to hunt for a bed in the neighbourhood of Ardgour.

The British Aluminium Company fixed upon the moorland at the head of Loch Leven, an arm of the sea to the south of Fort William, as a suitable place for the erection of their gigantic works. Water power had to be got from the lochs far up the valley on the wastes of the Black Mount. Here a huge dam was formed. The construction of the wall with sluices was on a scale similar to that at Aswan in Egypt. Native rock and concrete were employed. It took years to build. As the workmen had to reside on the spot, wooden huts were provided for their wives and families. But the education of the children had also to be seen to. It was inexpedient to build a school, so a sort of hall was used as a temporary schoolroom. To ascertain if the children taught by a young girl with a decided Cockney accent were being properly educated, a colleague and I were deputed to visit this almost inaccessible 'seminary.' This we did on 'a bright and cheerful afternoon towards the end of the merry month of June.' There were no roads. As far as the eye could reach were stretches of mountain and moor. Except by the narrow-guage railway that wound its way up the hills or by the trolley system used for conveying the bags of cement from the pier to the dam, there was no way of getting to the children. These bags were dropped into a suc-cession of hanging cradle-shaped buckets, which were attached at equal distances to an endless wire rope. This, supported on pulleys, kept slowly creeping over hill and dale. It was said, but I cannot vouch for the truth of it, that a Jew with a case of cheap jewellery, desirous of getting to the families at the dam, was advised by some practical joker at the pier to get into one of the buckets, when he would thus be sure of a free passage to his destination. He foolishly followed the advice. But he gave no consideration to time. When six o' clock came, and the men were leaving off work for the day, the gear stopped, with the result that he found himself suspended high above a valley, where he had to rest contented till the buckets began to move again on the following morning. This mode of transit, however, we eschewed, lest the fate of the son of Israel might be ours. An aeroplane was a *rara avis* in those days. It would have suited our purpose admirably, and we should have had the honour of being the first to make use of one to reach a school. The manager of the company, however, came to our assistance. He arranged for us to travel for so many miles at the start on a pug engine. Leaving it, we scrambled up a hill-face covered with boulders and heather for about eight hundred feet, till we came upon another pug engine, on the foot-plate of which we completed our journey. Having examined the children, we descended to Kinlochleven by the same engines. It was certainly a novel experience, and one never likely to occur again. As the day was intensely warm with brilliant sunshine, I found standing on the footplate behind the furnace getting too much for me, so for coolness I slipped along the side of the engine, and, holding on by the side rail, I drank in my fill of the vista of gorgeous scenery as we proceeded. I was reminded of the ratchet railways of the Swiss mountains, though no cog wheels were necessary, the gradients being inconsiderable. When at the dam we were pleased to find that the parents showed much solicitude for the education of their children. Here, as well as at

Kinlochleven, the workers had come from almost every corner of Great Britain and Ireland. In all my experience I never came across such a variety of dialects in so small an area, and that too where Gaelic was the language of the natives.

The foregoing narrative has dealt with visits to schools only, but I feel that I cannot conclude the chapter without placing on record the saddest journey I ever had to travel in the whole of my inspectorial career. It was as weird as it was painful. It occurred in the summer of 1889, in the height of the tourist season, when I was assisting the Inspector of the district in the examination of the schools on the west coast of Ross-shire. The latter, who had been in bad health for some time, died in Gairloch Hotel, which was then crowded with tourists. He had arrived on the previous evening, took seriously ill during the night, and passed away in presence of the local doctor in the forenoon of the following day. This alarmed the hotel manager, who naturally wished to keep the sad event from the visitors. Being associated with him, and on the spot, it fell to me to deal with the situation. After infinite trouble I made arrangements for removing the remains from the hotel that night about twelve o' clock, when there would be few persons about and all would likely be quiet. I had to take the body over thirty miles to Achnasheen Station on the Highland Railway, and thence by rail to Inverness. The only conveyance available was the large wagonette in which the Inspector had arrived on the previous evening. But the driver who was selected happened to be a true Celt, and for reasons which can easily be surmised, seemed disinclined to undertake the somewhat gruesome task of driving a wagonette and corpse such a distance in the still hours of the night. However, to dispel his scruples, I promised him 'a good time.' He understood what that meant, and on being assured that I would sit beside him, he risked facing all the other spirits his superstitious nature could conjure up.

On the stroke of twelve, in the presence of two or three local teachers, the coffin was roped into the wagonette, the head resting at the feet of myself and the driver. Unfortunately, at that very hour a violent thunderstorm was raging, with incessant flashes of lightning stabbing the darkness of the night. The rain came down in torrents; but the driver was well acquainted with the road, so we crept cautiously along at a walking pace. Our first halting-place was to be Kinlochewe Inn, where I had wired for a fresh pair of horses to be in waiting at 4 a.m. for the last stage of the journey. As we approached the inn the rain had ceased. The morning was balmy and sunny. Looking along the road in the direction of the inn I could detect no sign of life. This almost unnerved me, for I had to catch a train at Achnasheen at 6 a.m. Nor did the driver like the look of things. Relief soon came, however, for as we drew up a man leading a horse by each hand leisurely emerged from the stable. Needless to add, I completed the sad journey to Inverness without any untoward happening. It was an experience such as I am thankful to say I never had to undergo again.

Chapter V

TRAVELLING
BY SEA

Visiting schools by sea often entailed more exciting experiences than travelling by land. It also embraced a greater variety and number of risks; but these were inevitable, when the journeys had to be made in steamers and boats more or less seaworthy.

In 1883 the Inspector of the district and I paid our annual visit to all the schools on the west coast from Ullapool to Oban in a comparatively small racing yacht named the *Circe*. This was agreed to be the most convenient and comfortable method of getting from school to school along the coast. I have no doubt it was also the cheapest, otherwise the Department would not have sanctioned it. The yacht, which was used for the first time for this purpose, was hired from some one in Weymouth. A finer specimen of a racer, with its graceful lines and snow-white sails, could hardly be conceived. But accommodation was sacrificed to beauty. The cabin was small, and there were only two sleeping berths. An old English 'salt' with a long white beard, which reminded one of the Ancient Mariner, commanded the vessel. It was manned by two men—one the cook and handy man, the other the deck hand. As the old man was quite unacquainted with the west coast of Scotland, he was perpetually in a state of nerves. His temper often got the better of him. The two seamen, who dubbed him Sennacherib, probably because they detected his resemblance to this ancient potentate as depicted in a picture, detested him. The inspectorate had also frequently to thole at his lips more than was palatable. Through his ignorance of the coast and his unwillingness to study the charts, he nearly ran the yacht ashore at the entrance to Loch Torridon. But for me the most exciting trip was between Mallaig and the island of Eigg. At that time Mallaig was not a railway terminus nor the important place it now is. It consisted of a few houses occupied by crofters and fishermen and a small school taught by a Roman Catholic teacher. On the yacht besides myself were the Inspector's wife and sister, who occupied the berths, while I made myself as comfortable as the accommodation permitted in the cabin. My instructions were to proceed to Eigg early in the morning. Being anxious to carry them out, and knowing how long the journey would take, I rose at 4 a.m. and, proceeding on deck, roused Sennacherib. Like a Jack-in-the-box up from the forecastle hatch bobbed his head with the long white beard surmounted by a flowing red nightcap. The morning was wet and windy, with a heavy sea running. With a practised eye he surveyed the threatening aspect of the weather. I asked him if he considered it safe to attempt the journey. With a shrug of his shoulders he replied, "She'll go all right; but there won't be a dry skin on board." This was comforting indeed. But though his opinion was disconcerting, I was determined to risk the promised drenching. The hands were roused, the anchor weighed, a jib and reefed mainsail set, and out we went from the little sheltered bay into the open sea. The Captain steered, while I sat by him in the cockpit in a state of trepidation, which, however, I took good care to conceal. Unfortunately, the wind was freshening. The waves lashed against the rocky coast, and the yacht, well over on her beam ends, was tearing through the water like a knife. Having carefully studied the chart beforehand, I was convinced that we were keeping too near the coast. Excitement mastered me, so I ventured to express this opinion. As was his wont, the old man at once pooh-poohed my remark. I overheard him muttering *sotto voce* that he knew his work better than I, when Sam, the man on the bow, who was keeping a sharp lookout, suddenly shouted, "Rocks ahead, sir." I must admit I would hardly have believed it possible for a vessel to have sheered off to the starboard with such swiftness as the *Circe* away from the dark objects looming through the misty atmosphere in front. I gave a sigh of relief, for I knew the danger of striking a rock was past. It was now a case of tacking, with huge waves and spray continually sweeping over the narrow deck. After some hours Eigg was reached. Before going ashore I ascertained that the two ladies were so sick that they were unable to rise; but by the time I had examined the school they had almost recovered from their awful experience. That night in fairly calm weather we managed with a pilot on board to reach Arisaig, the approach to which from the sea is one of the most dangerous on the west coast.

The ill-feeling between Sennacherib and his crew became so acute, after the commission of the *Circe* expired, that it culminated in a sort of mutiny at Fort William. The latter in a state of intoxication made a murderous attack on the old man, with the result that they found themselves in prison. Thus ended an official cruise which from first to last provided one with a stomachful of stirring adventure.

In subsequent years we visited the west coast schools in a very seaworthy, roomy yacht named the *Snare*. It was chartered from Mr. Arthur Fowler of Braemore, son of Sir John Fowler of Forth Bridge fame, and was manned by Highland fishermen from Loch Broom. The Captain, who was acquainted with every inch of the coast from his boyhood, was a most reliable navigator. He seemed to possess a mysterious faculty for discovering relatives, mostly cousins far removed, in every other place at which we landed. But his knack of feeling 'a conviction of consanguinity' for the crofters with whom he foregathered, while the inspection of the school was proceeding, was sometimes the cause of much uneasiness, particularly when it was evident from his demeanour that he had been partaking rather liberally of the *usquebaugh* which in most cases had escaped excise duty, despite the vigilance of the peripatetic preventive men. Still, even in his elevated condition he insisted on handling the tiller himself. He would never allow anyone to usurp his function as Captain of the *Snare*. But, though we sometimes passed hours of anxiety when tacking near a reefy coast, his skill as a seaman never failed him. The cruise invariably ended without serious mishap.

Specially noteworthy were my trips to the small school

on the Monach Islands, popularly known to the Hebrideans as Heisker. They lie out in the Atlantic about nine miles off the coast of North Uist. In the latter part of last century no steamer called at these remote islands. The natives possessed large deckless boats in which they sailed to North Uist, or, as they called it, the Mainland, for supplies of provisions and peat for fuel. Of the four islands the largest, Ceann Ear, was the most fertile. On it the school was built beside the few houses of the inhabitants. To make the journey I had to hire a boat from a crofter at Paible, the nearest point on the coast of North Uist. As a rule the boat was old and inclined to leak. This made the passage through the great, green Atlantic rollers, which for ever dash against that coast, exceedingly risky at any time. As the pay was liberal, the boatmen, who were not too well-off, were only too willing to risk the 'riotous anger of the sea.'

On my first visit to the islands the boat, which carried two small sails attached to two short masts, was ballasted with big slabs of stone. This type of rig was considered safer than one big sail. I must confess I felt some uneasiness when I contemplated the huge, green, white-crested waves that were rolling shorewards and the amount of ballast intended to steady the frail-looking craft selected for the trip. However, it was useless to discuss the matter with the two hardy 'toilers of the sea,' who had made what they considered the best preparation possible both for their own safety and mine. As we ploughed through the waves every now and then, despite the most skilful steering, I was drenched when the boat happened to dip her bow into an oncoming wave and hesitated to rise freely to the next. When we had covered about five miles misfortune overtook us. The rudder, unable to withstand the strain, snapped. Luckily a small portion remained. With a presence of mind begotten of risks at sea, the steersman, seizing this, contrived, at great peril of falling overboard, to guide the boat to the landing-place. Alarmed at this mishap, I asked the men how we were to get back to North Uist. One of them replied, "Och, we will get a helm made while you are in the school." And sure enough they did; but who would guess what it was made of in an island where nothing resembling a tree was ever seen? Incredible as it may seem, it was made of good Spanish mahogany. However, the explanation was easy. On landing on Heisker one was surprised to see the numerous evidences of shipwrecks. For gates in the low, rude stone walls to keep out the cows, the beautiful cross-stick flooring of steamers was used, while cabers of teak, mahogany, and other valuable woods formed fittings for the houses. I also saw the brass-ringed port-hole of a large steamer doing service for a window frame in one house. One could not help noting the prosperous and healthy appearance of both old and young. I gathered that, like the natives of St. Kilda, they are very fond of their islands.

The inspection of the little school was an interesting task. The pupils, numbering fifteen, were nearly all fair-haired. From one year's end to the other they had never seen a stranger. Accordingly, it was not surprising that the youngest ones in particular were afflicted with shyness. At first I had the greatest difficulty in inducing them to look me straight in the face. In a little, however, by jocular remarks which provoked laughter I gained their confidence, and by the time the examination was concluded they were vieing with one another in their efforts to please me. Their knowledge of the outside world was wholly derived from books and pictures, supplemented by explanations from the teacher. They could only describe a horse from a picture, never having seen one in the flesh. They laughed heartily at the mention of a policeman, whom from a pictorial representation they looked upon as a sort of guy. The teacher, coming from an east coast county, knew no Gaelic. She was very earnest and capable. The results of examination were excellent. Here it is worthy of note that, when uniformity of tests in arithmetic all over Scotland was being discussed in the House of Commons, a member, taking extreme cases, pointed out how ridiculous it would be to expect the children in the remote island of Heisker to do the same sums as those in the best schools in Edinburgh. One hour was the statutory time allowed for the execution of the tests. Yet, if my memory does not err, it was recorded in the blue book of the following year that the Heisker pupils did all the sums correctly in three-quarters of an hour.

Next year I was deputed to visit the island officially, and again I was unfortunate in my weather. The outward journey was straight sailing; but whilst I was in the school the wind from a bad 'airt' began to freshen. The boatmen became anxious. One of them came twice to the door to enquire when I would be ready to leave. They knew the weather signs, and dreaded an exile of perhaps a week or more on the island, with no chance of letting their families know of their safety. But despite warning, and even threats, I did not take their prognostications seriously. On the point of my arrival the good people had handed to the teacher a huge lobster, fresh from the creel, for my consumption. I was fond of lobster, and was determined to sample it. As it was barely ready for eating when I had concluded the examination, at the suggestion of the teacher I strolled a few yards across to the west side of the island. I shall never forget the sad sight that met my eyes. The graves of shipwrecked sailors, little grassy mounds with nothing to indicate who they were or whence they came, were scattered everywhere. By the time I returned the lobster was cooked. Having partaken heartily of its most appetising parts, I hurried to the boat, where I found the men already seated and waiting for me. Now, tacking is a very tedious way of getting to one's destination. Therefore, as the wind necessitated this step, I coaxed them to sail straight across so as to land me on the coast of North Uist. Having done that, they could tack their way home to the north as best they could. During the passage I frequently heard them mention the word 'clach,' the Gaelic for stone. When we reached the coast, sure enough they landed me on a huge boulder. I have often regretted that I did not make a sketch of that stone in its native setting, for local tradition at least had it that on that very stone Prince Charlie landed when he first set foot on Scottish territory. I never had another opportunity of seeing it.

That same evening near sunset I climbed the hill behind the Established Church manse. From there I could descry far at sea my boatmen still tacking northwards. Glad was I that I had succeeded in reaching North Uist so easily. From this elevation I beheld for the first and last time many miles away the lonely saddle-shaped island of St. Kilda, with the needle-shaped Stacks of Bororay lying off its northern coast. The dark contours were beautifully and clearly silhouetted against the exquisite, golden western glow. I somehow felt like Moses viewing the promised land from the top of Pisgah.

Heisker one can never forget, with its solitary lighthouse, the erection of which at the time, I believe, caused much vexation to the natives, who were in the habit of deriving great benefit from occasional shipwrecks. I was told that shortly after the light was turned on for the first time a big steamer crashed on the rocks, the captain mistaking it for another light, probably that at the Butt of Lewis.

At the extreme south end of the Long Island, as the Outer Hebrides is called, lies the lonely island of Mingulay. At the time of my visit, more than forty years ago, it was inhabited by a few families living in a small hamlet consisting of some hut-like houses above a sandy beach on the north-east side. Behind this stretched a long, sloping grassy valley, rising to what looked like the summit of a hill, but which in reality was the top of a cliff rising about one thousand feet sheer from the Atlantic. Here innumerable sea-birds of various kinds found congenial nesting-places far from the disquieting blasts of passing steamers. Huge rolling waves from the Atlantic have been beating against its base from time immemorial. Protestantism never reached this remote isle. Every soul except the male teacher from the mainland was a Roman Catholic. The little elevated circular burying-ground, with its quaint home-made wooden crosses, bore evidence of this. The teacher in my time had been thirty years on the island. He had married a native, and had never left it. Far from the madding crowd he lived a contented life doing his duty. Nor did he ever wish 'to change his place.' I may here remark that it was often the case that once a teacher, who had probably married a Highland lass, became installed in such a school as this, he was seldom inclined to move south again. He became identified with local affairs, conducted prayer meetings, and even filled the pulpit in the absence of the minister. But woe betide the man who had no hobby to which to apply himself after school hours. The monotony of his life often resulted in a torpidity which occasionally adversely affected his teaching.

To reach Mingulay the Inspector had to sail about eighteen miles in an open boat from Barra. The landing was generally dangerous. When the wave lifted the boat up the face of the rock one had to seize the opportunity and leap ashore. If he missed his footing he would almost certainly have been drowned. Only an Inspector able to swim should have ever essayed to inspect the school on Mingulay. After partaking of the teacher's hospitality, one was always glad to take his departure as soon as possible. To-day, however, no risks need be run; for I am informed there is not a single inhabitant on this faraway island of the Western Seas. The cheery laugh of the children at play has given place to the screams of the sea-gulls and other aquatic birds. So much for Mingulay.

To reach North Uist from Benbecula the terrible winding North Ford had to be crossed. This is really a stretch of sands and treacherous quicksands some miles wide. At high tide the whole is completely covered with water. About the middle there is a channel, through which one can wade at lowest tide. But the crossing, though stones with seaweed attached mark the course, has always been dangerous. More than one person has lost his life by starting rather late from either side. When the traveller reached the channel and found it too deep to cross, he retraced his steps, only to find himself engulfed in some quicksand or overwhelmed by the incoming tide before he could reach the shore. I remember once crossing this ford on a moonlight night when the state of the tide made this possible. A man mounted on a white horse acted as guide. The scene was weird in the extreme. It was such as an emotional artist would have delighted to depict on canvas.

A steamer calling at an island without a pier had generally to cast anchor in a convenient small bay. A big boat rowed by hefty men then came alongside. Into it the passengers without respect of persons were bundled bag and baggage, after the cargo had been piled up so that the gunwale of the boat was sometimes only a few inches above the water. This was how the Inspector got ashore at such islands as Coll, Colonsay, Iona and the north end of Gigha.

Colonsay reminds me of a nasty crossing from that island to Port Askaig in the Sound of Islay. It was during a very stormy time of the year, when the nights were long and dark. The steamer due to call at the island at a certain hour in the evening arrived very late owing to rough weather. At the landing-place, in a shed lit by a solitary candle, I sat and shivered for some hours, eagerly listening for the sound of the siren proclaiming its arrival in the offing. When at last it did come I went out in a small boat, and, scrambling on board, discovered that I was not the sole passenger. Huddled up in a corner of the cabin was an old *cailleach* (woman), who had evidently joined the steamer at some Hebridean port of call. Whether this *compagne du voyage* was sick or merely pretending to be in distress did not occasion me much concern. It was on the verge of midnight. I sat for a time listening to the swish of the waves beating against the ribs of the steamer in the blackness without. The rolling and plunging almost sickened me. Suddenly the screw stopped. I sprang to my feet, knowing that in such a sea this indicated that something was wrong. Hurrying up the stairs I met the purser, who assured me that there was no danger. Intercepting my progress, he explained that the night being so stormy and dark the Captain was not quite sure of his bearings. Accordingly, he deemed it judicious to have the engines stopped till he could pick up the lighthouse on Rudha Mheal, the most northerly point of Islay. This was in a measure reassuring; but I did not feel inclined to retrace my steps to the cabin. I brushed past him, and, clinging to the sides of the open door of the deckhouse, I surveyed the waves lit up by the lights from the portholes. The vessel, not being under control, yawed here, there and everywhere. I was far from feeling comfortable every time she rolled into the trough of the waves.

> *Into the trembling billows of the main,*
> *Lord, Lord! methought what pain it was to drown.*

At last the Captain, who had never left the bridge, picked up the welcome light, and about 2.30 a.m. I landed at Port Askaig in sheets of rain and driving wind. With the collar of my coat pulled well up, I was hurrying along the pier, when a stooping old man with a white beard tapped my arm and asked if he could speak to me for a little. Not to be disobliging, and for the moment suspecting that what he wished to say might be of serious importance at such an unearthly hour, I asked him what he wanted. He thereupon blurted out that he had a grievance against the teacher of the school which his children were attending. As can easily be imagined, I was in the circumstances in no mood to lend an ear to parental troubles. I managed to put him off with an assurance that I would listen to his plaint in the morning. I hurried to the hotel, where I had warned the people to expect me, only to find everything in darkness. After no end of hammering on doors and windows I at last managed to arouse the landlord, who was profuse in apologies. Like others in similar circumstances, he wisely blamed the servants. Oh! these poor maids! How much they must thole when they know quite well they are not blameworthy. True to promise, I met my plaintiff after breakfast. I listened to his tale, and found that the teacher had justifiably expelled his children on account of their verminous condition. I rated him soundly for such a state of matters, and left him speechless, but no doubt wondering what, after all, Inspectors were really appointed for.

In the summer time the journey from Oban by one of the West Coast steamers to inspect the schools in the islands of Canna and Rhum generally proved a very pleasant outing. Owing to the nature of the course it took about two days and two night to complete the journey. On the first occasion a colleague and myself left Oban about 6 a.m. The steamer made direct for Castlebay in Barra, one of the most southerly of the Outer Hebrides. From there the course was to Lochboisdale in South Uist, Lochmaddy in North Uist, then across the Minch to Dunvegan in Skye, and thence southward to Canna, which was reached about 6 a.m., nearly twenty-four hours after leaving Oban. My colleague continued the journey to Rhum, the next place of call, while I landed at Canna to inspect the larger of the two schools. As this was the first time I had been there the pier-master had a lad of thirteen waiting to escort me to the school more than a mile away, which was not visible from the landing-place. As we rounded a corner of the little bay my guide, drawing my attention to the school, now plainly in view, exclaimed, "He's up. I see the smoke." For me this was good news, as I had to examine the children and catch another steamer about eight o'clock going to Oban in the reverse direction. As I approached the house, one end of which was the schoolroom and the other the teacher's residence, I was struck with the fine display of vegetables of all kinds in his garden. He told me he had once been a market gardener in England, and, noting the fertile soil of the island due to its trap formation, he started growing vegetables. What he produced, I am confident, would have done credit to any professional gardener. As the hour was so early, he asked me if I wished to partake of breakfast. I told him I had already had a cup of coffee, which the steward kindly prepared for me before going ashore. On his urging me to sample the oatcakes of his own baking, for he lived alone, I did so. While I sat devouring these, with a boiled fresh egg, washed down with a cup of excellent tea, in the apartment which paid the double debt of kitchen and sitting-room, he busied himself shaving and dressing in the adjoining bedroom. All the time, however, I was very uneasy, for I heard no sound of footsteps entering the lobby, which would indicate the arrival of pupils. When he emerged from his ablutions I remarked that I was afraid the children had failed to come out at such an unusual hour. With a casual "I'll soon see," he crossed the lobby, peeped into the classroom, and at once returned to tell me that the whole eighteen were sitting in readiness for me. The fact that everyone was barefooted accounted for the silence with which they had entered and taken their places. Some of the older ones were well over school age, and seemed much interested in their work. The infants, seated on a form at my back, persisted in making *sotto voce* personal remarks about the Inspector. Johnson is said to have called children 'pretty dears,' and to have given them sweets. By adopting the same tactics with the few confections I happened to have in my pocket as an antidote to possible sea-sickness, I managed to bribe them to silence. I noticed that each child had a religious badge of some sort pinned on the breast. The teacher explained that this had been supplied by a priest from Eigg on the previous Sunday. With the exception of the teacher and the proprietor's family all the inhabitants were Roman Catholics. Their chapel was the most prominent object on a treeless island. The examination being satisfactorily concluded, I caught the steamer, and, making the return journey by the same route, reached Oban on the following day.

I should mention that as we steamed along the coast of Skye I descried a solitary sheep half-way up on a small green patch on the face of a cliff at least four hundred feet high. As a lamb it must have fallen without much injury from the top, and found footing where it could neither get up nor down. It could be seen from the sea only. Next year I saw it on the same ledge. It was hopeless to attempt to rescue it alive. How it subsisted year in year out on the scanty grass, which was just visible, was a mystery. All the same, the patch may have been larger than it looked; and no doubt the excrement of sea birds may have added to the fertility of what little soil there was. Anyhow, there the poor creature was marooned, awaiting the day when it would doubtless form a meal for the voracious seagulls or eagles.

When I visited Canna next year I was startled to find the teacher sullen, depressed and blear-eyed. He had a sad tale to tell. For more than a week he had been without sleep owing to acute tooth-ache. In such an island no cure was available, so he had just to thole. When I told him I carried in my bag, which I had left in the piermaster's shed, a tube of carbolic jelly, which I assured him would effect a cure provided the decayed tooth had a cavity large enough to contain it, his face lightened up, and he became more talkative. The examination concluded, in his hurry to secure my panacea he insisted on rowing me in his own boat to the pier. To walk round the bay would have taken longer. To my great delight I found the tube. Had I not done so my regret would have been deep, for on my handing it to him he clutched it with both hands as if it were the greatest treasure on earth. He was still volubly thanking me as I boarded the steamer, which had just drawn up alongside the little pier. Whether or not he found the relief which I predicted I cannot tell. It was the last time I visited Canna.

Chapter VI

HOSPITALITY

Highland hospitality has for centuries been a byword, but perhaps the trend of modern civilisation has rendered it less common and less necessary than it used to be. Half a century ago the school Inspector was a welcome sojourner in the home of the landed proprietor or the clergyman. Here his presence and conversation formed an agreeable variant in the diurnal monotony where solitude reigned and the turmoil of teeming cities had no disturbing influence. The date of inspection being intimated beforehand, there was ample time for preparation adequate to the importance of his visit.

In those days whisky, without which Highland hospitality would have been an empty sound, was both plentiful and cheap. Perhaps it may make a toper sigh for 'the good old days' to read this. When staying in a Highland hotel the Inspector was almost certain to be offered a glass of whisky before breakfast by some drouthy member of the School Board who dropped in with Paul Pry's polite 'I hope I don't intrude.' A little later, on the verge of leaving for a school many miles distant, he had a chance of being offered a second glass as a fortification for the journey. On his arrival at the school he was met by the teacher, who, commenting on the long drive, or possibly the trying atmospheric condi-

tions, did not fail to suggest a stimulant to restore the circu-
lation. Whether it was accepted or not, he no doubt
inwardly hoped that the offer would put the Inspector in
good humour, and thereby temper with mercy the ordeal to
which his pupils were about to be subjected. If the examination was protracted, a pause in the work was deemed
necessary to let the examinees get a breathing space and
much needed 'piece.' And what was more natural than that
the Inspector should go into the schoolhouse for a sip of
something to sustain him for the remainder of the examination. This completed, an adjournment was as a rule made to
the teacher's house or the manse for lunch. Here the usual
appetiser was proffered. More liquor was on the table to
wash down the roast beef and greens; and it would have
been insulting to his host if the Inspector left without a
deoch-an-doruis (stirrup cup). Nor did the day's temptation
end there. It was indeed an inhospitable region where some
member of the School Board did not turn up in the course
of the evening to have a friendly glass or two, and a crack
with the Inspector on things in general and education in
particular. Thus the day often passed with temptations
which took a determined character to resist. To-day the
Inspector motors from school to school practically unrecog-
nised by the general public. When necessity compels him to
put up at a hotel he can sit there after the day's work is done
smoking a pipe of peace as he sips his lemonade or other
non-intoxicating beverage, and meditates on the number of
times he sliced his ball or bungled an easy putt at the last
hole during the afternoon's round of golf with a local novice,
whom he could easily have beaten had he concentrated his

mind more on the game and less on the scenic environment of the course.

While I am on the subject of spirituous liquor, I may be excused for writing something on smuggling, which was only too common in the Highlands fifty years ago. I learned a good deal about illicit distillation from various sources. I even saw the interior of a bothy where the smugglers were busy making the vile stuff. It came about in this way. One winter evening I was sojourning in an Established Church manse in a district of the Highlands which had the reputation of being a hotbed of smuggling. I evinced such an interest in the process that the minister said if I was anxious to see it he believed he could gratify my wish. Being by nature of an artistic turn, I conjured up in my mind a scene which I might find pleasure in depicting at some future time. Accordingly, I sprang up, and, buttoning myself into a heavy coat, accompanied his Reverence to the kitchen, where his 'man' was seated by the fire smoking a clay pipe and reading what looked like a Bible. On the minister asking him if he thought Black Angus was busy that night, he replied that he believed he was. It was there and then arranged that, as there was no risk of betrayal on my part, he should guide me to the bothy. The night was exceedingly cold and dark, and, as my companion alleged, very suitable for smuggling. At a point we left the highway and crossed a stretch of boggy moorland with no track whatever. Now and again I could just discern what appeared to be big dark objects of some kind. Coming to a halt, my guide, peering into my face, asked me if I had detected the smugglers' den. On my assuring him that I had not, he whispered an expression of satisfaction. We then retraced our steps, and about fifty yards from where we halted he drew a sheet of coarse sacking from the end of what I took to be a peat stack, when I beheld two men seated by a fire over which the distilling kettle was suspended. Naturally, they were startled at the sight of a stranger; but a few words in Gaelic from my guide put them so much at their ease that they readily explained the simplicity of the process without any reference to its illegal aspect. On departing I am afraid I offended them by refusing to sample the product of their primitive still. I hope none of my readers will set me down as *particeps criminis* in keeping my secret to myself.

And here let me state that smuggling would have been more common than it was but for the cost of the appliances, and particularly the copper worm necessary for distillation. I heard of a Loch Carron smith who contrived to make the worm by filling a tube with a small shot and plugging both ends. He then wound it round a piece of tree trunk, removed the plugs, ran off the lead, and the worm was complete.

It must be borne in mind that the clandestine making of whisky, though a breach of the man-made law, was not considered by Highlanders in general inconsistent with the tenets of the decalogue. Even men in position sometimes connived at it. A well known and much respected factor on a Highland estate once presented me with a bottle of smuggled whisky, clear as water, as I was leaving his house after partaking of a sumptuous lunch. I accepted it as a curio to convince some friends in Aberdeenshire that illicit distillation was still practised in certain Highland districts. But they never saw or sampled it, for the bottle was accidentally smashed inside the travelling rug in which I had wrapped it.

I was once examining the small school of Alligin in Wester Ross, when a barefooted girl of thirteen entered, bearing on her back a lame little sister, whom she had carried some miles across a trackless moor. As I was questioning the highest class in history, Mr. Darroch, the proprietor of Torridon, was standing by my side. The incidents connected with the Porteous Riots cropped up. Forgetful for the moment that the natives of Alligin were notorious smugglers, I was questioning the pupils on the nature of smuggling, when smiles took the place of answers. The pupils whose relatives had to do with it blushed scarlet, and no doubt the laird, though he never let on, noted this. He was a keen abstainer, and never scrupled to evict a tenant found guilty of smuggling.

Hospitality extended to the Inspector visiting a school in an island where there was no inn was always exceedingly welcome. I have in mind the small island of Gometra, lying off the larger island of Ulva, on the west coast of Mull. Here I always received a warm welcome. The kindness was unstinted, and the scenery entrancing in its solitude and picturesqueness. But sadness invariably oppressed me as I crossed Ulva. On every hand scattered along the eight miles of rough road were the ruins of many houses, which had at one time been occupied by a considerable population. An evil fate had overtaken them. For some reason or other the crofters had been evicted. After enduring the greatest hardships, they had mostly to seek asylum in Canada, where, like those similarly treated in Strathnaver in Sutherlandshire, they and their descendants were said to have prospered. The evictions in Ulva must have been fraught with the invocation of many curses and no end of heart-burning. As I drove along I could not help repeating Goldsmith's lines on the 'Deserted Village':

> *But now the sounds of population fail;*
> *No gentle murmurs fluctuate on the gale;*
> *For all the blooming flush of life has fled, etc.*

The proprietor of Gometra once told me an incident which showed that in certain circumstances a breach of the law may be overlooked. A native told him one morning that a boatload of men were busy with a net poaching salmon on the coast of his island. After breakfast, he interviewed them. The leader explained that, hearing that salmon were plentiful about Gometra, they had come there to spend a holiday and have an enjoyable time. Despite threats of prosecution and the severest penalties, the invaders refused to quit the place. Of course they knew that there was no policeman within many miles of the island. Finally, the proprietor left them in disgust. Let me quote his own words as to the result. "The fact is, as I never did any fishing myself, I let them fish there as long as they liked, for almost every morning they aimed at propitiating me by handing in to my wife a liberal share of the spoils with their compliments." Viewing their conduct in the light of obvious bribery, he laughed heartily. But these poachers found that they could not pursue their game with impunity on every coast. Attempting it once too often nearer civilisation, they were caught and heavily fined.

When visiting Tomatin School in the Culloden district, I sometimes spent an evening with Mr. McDougall, the factor. In the days of the Rebellion of 1745 this was a hot Jacobite corner. Half a century ago unrecorded local tales connected with the rising were plentiful. The factor knew not a few. As illustrating the reward for saving a life, he told me that his grand-uncle fought at Culloden on the side of the Prince. During the rout of the rebel army a neighbour of his was being hotly pursued by a redcoat on the left bank of the River Nairn. His grand-uncle, who chanced to be on the other side, seeing his friend's danger, levelled his rifle, and by good luck shot the pursuer. When the man turned and saw his enemy dead he shouted across the river in Gaelic, "I will be giving you two days at the peats for that." He must have been a humorist, promising on the spur of the moment without seriously estimating its sufficiency such a recompense as a reward for life saving. Again, there lived in that neighbourhood to a good old age a tailor known as Cripple Noble. I was told that his defect came about in this way. As a small urchin he happened to be herding his mother's cow close to Culloden. Seeing the armies gathering, curiosity prompted him to creep as near as possible to the field of fray. After the debacle, when men and horses were rushing in every direction, in a state of terror he lay flat on his face amongst the heather. An English dragoon sweeping along noticed him, and, slowing down, with his sword cut a small slice off his hip just below the kilt, thus rendering him lame for the rest of his life. Traditions connected with Culloden will die hard. To glean them one has to linger for some time in the neighbourhood.

I once stayed a night in Skibo Castle before the well-known philanthropist, Andrew Carnegie, purchased the estate. In the course of the evening my hostess showed me to a bedroom on the ground floor which I was to occupy. It seemed rather dark, due to the comparatively small window and the unusual thickness of the walls. Perhaps gathering from my looks as well as from the absence of remarks that I was not at all taken with it, she proceeded to inform me, with what truth she did not know, that this was the very room in which the celebrated Marquis of Montrose slept on his way to Edinburgh, where he was executed, on the 21st May, 1650, after being treacherously delivered into the hands of David Lesley by Macleod of Assynt. As may be imagined, this interesting piece of historical information was not conducive to sound sleep. I conjured up all sorts of scenes. I pictured the abject, determined, revengeful captive lying there with armed men guarding the door. Then Ayton's lines were forcibly brought home to me:

Come hither, Evan Cameron,
Come, stand beside my knee, etc.

At Rothiemurchus in Inverness-shire for years I found a congenial friend in the Rev. Donald McDougall, the parish minister. Many a pleasant walk and interesting conversation we had of an evening as we sauntered through the pine woods by the famous Loch an Eilean. From the shore opposite Lochindorb Castle, the retreat of the notorious Wolf of Badenoch, we often watched the ospreys fishing. It was exceedingly interesting to observe one of these comparatively rare birds of the eagle species swoop down and, as it skimmed the surface of the water, seize in its talons, seemingly without pause or effort, some unwary trout that happened to be swimming near the surface. The victim it bore aloft to the rough-looking heap of twigs forming its eyrie on a corner at the top of the castle ruins. My companion informed me that one year two females arrived with the male bird. They fought with one another for days, till one night the local gamekeeper happened to see the victor hold her wounded rival below the water till life was extinct.

One always appreciated kindness bestowed from an unexpected quarter. One winter I was staying for a few nights in Bridgend Hotel in Islay. The wife of the proprietor of Dunlossit in the north end of the island was entertaining a number of the leading natives. As the large dining-room was to be occupied, I had to take up my quarters in a small, comfortable parlour upstairs. Early in the evening the good lady, having heard that I was sitting there all alone, although a complete stranger, came to me and insisted that I should join the happy throng downstairs, adding at the same time that my so doing would enhance her own happiness. Apparelled as I was I had some hesitation in complying with her kind request; but her thoughtfulness impressed me, so down I went and along with the others spent a most enjoyable evening.

When I think of Islay I see Port Ellen, where I had

occasion to be during the Great War when the *Tuscania*, with thousands of American soldiers, had just been torpedoed by a German submarine off the south coast with terrible consequences. Two rafts of curious construction lay stranded on the sandy beach in front of the hotel. A series of loops of rope with small globular wooden floats was attached to each side. A soldier clutching one of these could keep himself afloat till rescued. The bodies washed ashore were collected and buried in a fenced piece of grassy sward about a mile to the west of the village. To-day, however, all the little mounds save one have disappeared. The remains were disinterred and taken to America, so that the spot can hardly now be called a God's Acre.

At almost every visit to the South Uist schools the Inspector of the district and I were hospitably entertained in the manse at Druimsdale by the much respected Established Church minister and his family. The manse was in reality a large farm-house, to which a huge acreage, including Heckla, the highest mountain in the island, was attached. The daughters were well educated and very musical. With various forms of entertainment, in which the singing of Gaelic songs in congenial surroundings formed an essential part, the time passed all too quickly. Sitting by the drawing-room window within sound of the glorious Atlantic rollers breaking on the western shore, one could easily imagine himself there in the time of Prince Charlie, gazing at the armed brig *Dutillet*, with him on board, cruising off the coast of Wice, the name which Durbé, the French writer, thinks applied to the whole of the Outer Hebrides. Sunday came with its indescribable calm and brilliant sunshine. For some reason which escapes my memory, service was to be conducted by a missionary in a crofter's cottage, about two miles along the shore, instead of in the Parish Church. Our little band proceeded along the hard white sands, on which the sun was shining with dazzling effect. Arrived at the place of worship, we found that the service had just commenced. It was in Gaelic, and could only be described as primitive in its simplicity. One was struck with the tone of intense earnestness and devotion that prevailed. I reflected that at that very hour service was being conducted in St. Giles' in Edinburgh, where, after all, the song of praise, accompanied on the great sounding organ, was not more acceptable to Almighty God than the beautiful psalm commencing:

> *I love the Lord because my voice*
> *And prayer he did hear.*

in Gaelic:

> *Is toigh leam Dia, airson gu'n d'eisd*
> *Rim' ghuth, 's ri m' urnuigh fos,*

sung from the heart in that little thatched cottage to the tune of Dundee without any instrumental accompaniment.

That Sunday forenoon as we were leaving the manse we saw numbers of Roman Catholics going to service in their chapel. It seems not to be generally known that a considerable proportion of the inhabitants of the Outer Hebrides, south of Harris, are adherents of the Church of

Rome. Their ancestors in these remote islands, undisturbed by the turmoil of the Reformation, maintained a creed which dated back to the ancient Celtic Church. Here proselytising is unknown. Roman Catholics and Protestants live in perfect harmony.

Writing of proselytising, I am reminded of a letter which appeared in the *Glasgow Herald* during the Great War. A considerable number of lasses had come from Uist to Glasgow to take part in the lucrative work of shell filling at Georgetown. The writer who had evidently been informed that priests had been seen in touch with these strangers, ignorant of the circumstances, concluded that they were endeavouring to win them over to the Church of Rome. Familiar as I was with the Hebrides, I knew only too well that the clergy of their denomination were simply looking after the spiritual welfare of their own flock, as they are in duty bound to do. That these healthy, guileless girls, far away from home, should be subjected to the snares and temptations of a great city like Glasgow made the supervision of them by the priests all the more essential. Of course the writer, whoever he was, put pen to paper in sheer ignorance. I expected a letter of contradiction, but none appeared. Perhaps the editor grasped the absurdity of the allegation and cut off the correspondence.

Chapter VII

SCHOOL BOARD MEMBERS

In the days of School Boards the members considered themselves men of importance, as doubtless they were. As a rule at first the 'well-to-do' chiefly aspired to the office. Later the much respected tradesman found a place alongside the landed proprietor and minister. Not infrequently he begrudged the teacher his remuneration simply because it exceeded his own earnings. But parsimoniousness was not confined to plebeians. The affluent member was often more concerned in keeping down the school rate than in the education of the children. A story went round that at a meeting of a country Board the latest report on the school was about to be read by the clerk, when a wealthy farmer struck in with, "Never mind the report, mister; what's the siller?" After all, it was quite immaterial which of the two things should be dealt with first, as a favourable report was the index of a good grant and *vice versa*. As might be expected, the stingy type of member was a thorn in the side of the teacher should the grant for some reason or other not come up to expectation. Gaelic-speaking members in some parts of the Highlands wisely refrained from making entries in the school log book. Some, however, through their ignorance of English, betrayed their officiousness by writing comments bristling with bad spelling and worse grammar. The Inspector might smile and have his thoughts as he read them; but the criticism which the teacher expected was never forthcoming. What could the Inspector do or say? The law allowed the member to make entries; at least, it did not forbid him to do so.

Laughable incidents occasionally occurred to enliven School Board meetings. What follows was communicated to me by the reverend chairman of a School Board in the Highlands. One member, accustomed to demand value for his money, belonged to the class of sheep farmers. His knowledge of English was as scant as it was inaccurate; but the Gaelic he had imbibed with his mother's milk was unimpeachable. The appointment of a female assistant who could benefit the community by teaching the piano was under discussion. When challenged for his opinion this worthy objected to the proposal in these words: "I will not be voting for a woman that spends her time playing on a 'guano.'" Nevertheless, the lass with the piano received the appointment.

The most unbearable of all was the bumptious member. He was disliked by the teachers, commanded no respect, and got little consideration from the Inspector. One Highland landlord of my acquaintance, who was chairman of an important School Board, might be placed in this category. In his young days he had been an officer either in the army or navy, I forget which. Anyhow, his career had ingrained in him a feeling that his presence wherever he went demanded subservience. He seemed to be so obsessed with his own supreme importance that when he vouchsafed to shake hands, which he rarely did, he offered the first two fingers of his right hand. The gentlemanly Inspector of the district naturally resented this on his meeting him for the first time. But, 'once bitten, twice shy,' next time they met they both shook fingers.

This same autocrat once accompanied me into a classroom where the infants were being taught by a very modest but capable mistress. When we entered she was busy teaching an object lesson on the lion. I begged her to continue. To illustrate the lesson she was making use of a card having on one side a picture of the animal. When she had finished, this slave of his own importance put out his hand for the picture, which he wished to examine. The teacher, thinking he meant to shake her hand, extended it. Much to her obvious discomfiture and my disgust, he at once withdrew his. She blushed scarlet to the very roots of her hair. I was very sorry for her. I am sure no teacher under his jurisdiction grieved when he ceased to visit the schools in the district.

After the conclusion of a day's work it was always a form of relaxation to converse with a scholarly member of the School Board. The Rev. David Ferguson, minister of the *quoad sacra* parish of Kinlochluichart, was a man in whose company one could always spend an enjoyable evening. He was a bachelor of great literary attainments. His knowledge of the classics was remarkable; but only his most intimate friends knew this, for he was the last man in the world to make any display of his learning. The nature of his parish, chiefly moorland, with few inhabitants, enabled him to devote much time to study, to which he was naturally inclined. He became a personal friend and favourite of the cultured Lady Ashburton, proprietrix of the estate, chiefly on account of his unassuming manner and scholarship. In her mansion amongst persons of note with whom he had foregathered was Thomas Carlyle. I got it from a neighbouring minister that he used to make the Sage of Chelsea prick up his ears when at table he quietly capped some learned remark with an apt classical quotation. He himself told me he one day induced the great writer to mount the pulpit when he accompanied him to see the interior of his church. On his soliciting a few words of comfort, as he put it, from Thomas behind the book-board, the latter only shook his head and said, "Na, na preachin' was never in my line." He also told me something of the private life of the Sage while he sojourned at Kinlochluichart. After dinner he would quietly withdraw from the cackle of the drawing-room, which seemed to bore him. Later, when all the guests had taken their departure and stillness prevailed, he would almost stealthily re-enter the room where her ladyship sat expecting him. There as he lay on the hearthrug, leaning his elbow on a hassock in front of the fire, he entered into learned discussions with her till far into the morning. On these occasions he was never without his faithful companion, his clay pipe, the smoke of which he kept puffing up the chimney. But both kindred souls have many years ago passed to their account.

Half a century ago there was a wide distinction between the Established and Free Churches, the two predominant ecclesiastical bodies in Scotland. Adherents of the

former were called Moderates. No love was lost between
the members of the two denominations. A considerable
number of the Highland Free Church ministers could then
only be described as bigots. The farther removed their field
of ministration was from populous centres the keener
seemed to be their religious convictions. The more narrow-
minded ones assumed a Pharasaic sourness in their
demeanour. They also adopted a 'holier-than-thou' attitude
towards the Moderates, who, however, did not as a rule give
much heed to their pious idiosyncrasies, though they
sometimes sneered at them. These bigots looked with
horror on the singing of hymns and paraphrases in church.
For them the Psalms of David were enough. All else was the
carnal work of man, with which, according to them, the
devil was well satisfied. An organ in church they execrated
in no measured language. It was facetiously dubbed 'a kist
o' whustles.' For many years after the Disruption musical
instruments found no place in the Free Churches. Even the
most learned and enlightened of the clergy viewed their
introduction as an aid to singing as sacrilege. Well do I
remember sitting on a Sunday evening in the church of the
father of Professor Robertson Smith. The precentor had
introduced a small organ for the first time. Where it came
from or where it ultimately found a resting-place I could
never find out. Anyhow, there it was in front of him. As the
reverend Doctor passed up to the pulpit his eye caught sight
of the instrument. He halted and, pointing a finger at it, said
in a peremptory tone, "Put that thing outside at once."
Needless to say, his order was immediately obeyed. Now
listen to this. In the *Life* of the distinguished professor,

published by Adam & Charles Black (p. 558), it is recorded that on the way to Keig churchyard his coffin was borne into his father's church, where he was the first to be baptised. After the benediction it was again lifted, *while the Dead March in Saul was played*. What a change!

But let me revert to the clergy of the Highlands and Islands. Several of the Free Church ministers strongly denounced the teaching of songs in the public schools. To do so was little short of a sin. One man, a member of an insular School Board, as genial and kindly a soul as one could wish to meet, carried his bigotry so far as to order the teachers to cease the teaching of carnal songs in school. Non-musical, lazy teachers would have been only to glad to comply with his injunction. As it happened, one poor female, fond of music and anxious to brighten her work with an occasional song, was particularly hard hit. At my visit, not knowing the state of matters, I asked her to let me hear her pupils sing their favourite song. I can yet see her as she told me with tearful eyes and quivering lip that the Rev.—, of whose church she was a member, had forbidden her to teach Singing. When the injunction was first laid on her, for advice she wrote her father, who was an elder in a large city church in the south. Naturally, he told her to teach Singing, adding that there was surely some reason other than a sanctimonious one for such an unconscionable injunction. On this she recommenced the teaching, and, lo! the result. The minister carried his vindictiveness so far as to refuse her the privileges to which she was entitled according to the rites of the Church.

The principal school in this minister's parish was taught

by a Moderate who had the reputation of having 'a bee in his bonnet.' As he taught carnal songs in school, his Reverence was never tired of denouncing him. One day the latter during a visit to the school expressed a hope that the pupils were not being taught carnal songs. "Not at all," said the teacher. "Stand, children; we are going to let the minister hear 'Scots wha hae.'" This was enough. His Reverence, deeply shocked, donned his satin hat and at once made for the door. The sequel was that at next Board meeting he spent much valuable time dilating on the great sin of teaching such songs in school. But luckily his fellow-members did not see eye to eye with him on the matter. His threats carried weight with the teachers of his own persuasion only. But he was only one of many who could not tolerate the singing of songs in school.

In those days it was difficult for the Highland mind to reconcile gaiety and piety, amusement and religion. A story is told of a minister who enlisted the aid of the local factor to stop a young man from playing profane music on a fiddle. Instead of having the instrument confiscated and burned, the sympathetic factor rewarded the fiddler with half a crown for his skill in playing his favourite strathspey, the 'Reel o' Tulloch.' Over this the wrath of the minister may be more easily imagined than described.

Let me here record what I believe is a 'chestnut.' A young lad was one Sunday accompanying an elder to church. After covering some miles in silence he ventured to say, "It's a very beautiful day." "Indeed," said the elder, "but is this a day to be speaking about days?" The reproof implied that it was an act of impiety even to refer to atmospheric conditions on the Sabbath day.

I once saw a curious and most unexpected sidelight thrown on a very narrow-minded Free Church minister's character. To some of my readers, and particularly teetotal ones, what I am about to relate may seem almost incredible. It is nevertheless true. It happened on the day of the inspection of a school not a hundred miles from Inverness. In the examination the minister took a special interest, chiefly because both the teacher and the bulk of the children's parents were connected with his church. He waited till the work was finished and the school closed for the day. Then along with myself and two or three other members of the Board he accepted the teacher's invitation to lunch in the schoolhouse. According to custom, the teacher, who was a Highlander born and bred, before proceeding with the meal filled with whisky the requisite number of glasses on the table. When hands were being unceremoniously extended for the much needed refreshment, the white-haired clergyman rose, and, raising his hand, invoked a blessing on the liquor, as if it were one of the special gifts of the Creator. While he did this I noticed that the attitude of the members, with their closed eyes and bowed heads, was one of becoming reverence. No doubt this aged and much respected minister would have heartily endorsed every word of what the famous surgeon, Lord Dawson of Penn, said when the Liquor (Popular Control) Bill was introduced. "Fermented liquor," he said, "could not in his opinion be banished from modern civilisation. Drinking was part and parcel of the existence of people in their private and public life. It was even a sacred problem, used as such in the Christian faith."

It was more than likely that on account of that blessing the old man rose, rather than fell, in the esteem of his elders. Of one thing I am certain. The Moderate minister fond of a seasonable glass, facetiously referred to as 'the Auld Kirk,' would no more have dreamed of asking a blessing over it than he would have thought of committing suicide. However, the blessing appeared in no way to detract from the potency of the liquor. It seemed rather to add to it, to judge from the subsequent loquacity of more than one member who had hitherto been keeping a 'calm sough.'

Dealing in spirituous liquors was sometimes curiously blended with piety. To quote an instance: The innkeeper at Auchnasheen, good man, invariably closed his bar while he conducted family worship in the back parlour.

But while some of the Free Church clergy wore an air of piety, sometimes supplemented by a sanctimonious whine, their words and actions were frequently apt to betray a lack of sincerity. The sayings of some were not devoid of humour. I recall the day I travelled in the same compartment of a Highland Railway train with a leading Free Church minister of great reputation as a preacher. Seated beside him was a girl who had evidently come a long way, for she looked tired. After a little she fell asleep, while his Reverence and a friend carried on an animated discussion of the Declaratory Act, at that time a bone of contention. As we neared Inverness the girl awoke, and as she rubbed her eyes she accidentally nudged his Reverence with her elbow. On this he began to talk to her, and, if I remember rightly, the conversation turned upon her occupation and where she came from. Anyhow, he said laughingly, as he looked towards his ministerial companion, "Well, well, you can tell your mistress that you were sleeping beside the Rev. —." The inference conveyed by his statement was obvious. Knowing the esteem in which his congregation held him, I was much surprised. From his point of view it was a capital joke; from mine it was a revelation.

Occasionally a reverend member of a School Board would show lamentable ignorance of what should be familiar to any intelligent University-bred man. I was once examining the senior pupils of a country school in a sparsely populated district. By my side, evidently an interested listener, stood the Free Church clergyman of the district. The pupils having recited Portia's speech from *The Merchant of Venice*, I proceeded to test their grasp of the sentiments it conveyed. For the benefit of his Reverence, as much as out of respect for the cloth, I am afraid I did not fail to enlarge upon the beauty of the lines. As the pupils were being dismissed he quietly asked me who wrote such a beautiful passage. I was so taken aback by his ignorance that I simply said "Shakespeare." I have not the least doubt, provided he possessed a copy, one would have found him that night engrossed in hunting through some play of the bard of Avon for gems of thought which he would never have conceived possible to occur in anything associated with the theatrical profession.

The minister of any denomination who showed sincerity in his convictions, with which one might disagree, always commanded a measure of respect. On the other hand, the man whose hypocrisy was obvious was looked upon with contempt. One reverend member of an important School Board in a Lowland parish, who was always present when the school was being inspected, contrived to hoodwink his congregation for a number of years. But he was found out at last. He generally joined the Inspectors at lunch at the hospitable board of another wealthy member. He posed every time as a total abstainer, and with upturned nose and averted eyes invariably passed the wine decanter without helping himself to its contents. The Inspector of the district used to express to me his high opinion of this man's principles and moral character. Personally, for some instinctive reason I had my doubts, though to please him I verbally agreed with him. But the climax came when this much respected ecclesiastic was found one Saturday night intoxicated by the roadside not many miles from his manse. The tidings spread like wildfire. The bulk of his congregation was inclined to disbelieve the evil report, especially when he appeared in the pulpit next day and excelled himself in the eloquence of his discourse. Ultimately, however, all were convinced that the report was only too true. Evidence came to hand which proved that he had been leading a Jekyll and Hyde life for a number of years. He left the country and sought asylum in a colony where his previous career was not likely to be known, and if known, probably disbelieved, for he was one of the most fawning and plausible of men. But the case was very exceptional, and I am bound to admit that amongst ministers of the Free Church, in which I was brought up, I had some of my most cherished and confidential friends. To-day, 'though lost to sight, they are still to memory dear.'

The members of the School Board and the teacher did not always see eye to eye. There were various reasons for the lack of harmony. Let me give an illustration of a case in which this was inevitable. I was conducting the examination of a school in the Black Isle, a district of Easter Ross. Most of the members of the Board were of the farming class. It being the winter time, when outdoor work was at a stand-still, there was a full muster present in the schoolroom. The completed official schedules and forms were lying on the teacher's desk. One of them contained a list of pupils withheld from examination on account of some mental defect or ailment. One farmer lifted this sheet and began to scrutinise it. Suddenly his face grew red. Its expression changed from complacency to wrath. With compressed lips, and form in hand, he approached the teacher, who had entered the name of his son as being withheld on account of weak intellect. The fat was in the fire. I distinctly heard the parent in a towering passion exclaim, "My laddie's nae daft. There's naething wrang wi' him mair nor you." But the teacher was obdurate. He had his own reason for thinking otherwise; so, despite the risk of subsequent animosity, the laddie's name remained on the form. A painful situation such as this could not arise nowadays.

From a clergyman in Ballachulish, who was a member of the School Board and always full of humour, I heard the following tale connected with the district. In Loch Leven, opposite the slate quarries, lies a small island on which is a burying-ground. Here on dark nights a weird light, locally known as the 'licht,' is often seen to rise above the graves and float slowly in the direction of Glencoe, as if it were the ghost of some restless victim of the massacre. When the minister came to the district he was informed of this terrifying apparition by a member of his congregation, whom he instructed to let him know at any hour of the night when the 'licht' was on the move. He had not long to wait, for that night about twelve o'clock the man, in a state of intense trepidation, roused him, and forthwith led him to a safe spot from which the spectre was visible. And, indeed, there was no mistaking it as it moved backwards and forwards along the distant hillside. About a week afterwards the minister happened to be visiting some members of his congregation in that neighbourhood, and judiciously combining the secular with the sacred, he heard a complaint from one poor crofter that, as there was no fence separating his holding from the far-stretching heathery mountainside, he had recently lost a fine ewe, and that although he and his wife, carrying a lighted lantern, had made a diligent search, they had failed to recover the missing member of the flock. The minister, hearing the full details, had no difficulty in concluding that the 'licht' he had seen was that issuing from the crofter's lantern, but for private reasons he wisely kept the secret to himself. However, I had it from a reliable source that a light is undoubtedly visible in certain atmospheric conditions. Even Andrew Lang had seen it, and considered it a suitable theme for his pen. Scientists explain it as a phosphorescent emanation from the graveyard known as marsh gas, but recognised by the superstitious as 'Will-o'- the wisp.'

A well known Established Church minister once made me laugh over an incident connected with a leading member of his School Board who was one of his elders and farmed a considerable acreage in the parish. Since he cultivated his glebe and reared his own stock, it was customary for the minister to attend the annual local fair. On the occasion referred to he came across his esteemed church supporter having a heated quarrel with another farmer, evidently due to their having been imbibing too freely. His Reverence — a big, burly Highlander — in virtue of his cloth, deemed it necessary to step between them. Seizing his elder by the coat collar and holding him at arm's length, he said in an assumed pious tone, "Now, Colin, remember what Christ said. If thine enemy smite thee on the one cheek turn to him the other also." But the irate Colin was in no mood to follow this divine injunction. Pushing the minister aside, he shouted loud enough to be heard half across the market stance, "Awa' wi' yer Christian blether, minister. Moses is the man for me; an eye for an eye and a tooth for a tooth," and he once more went for his adversary. In those days in outlying places it was too often the case that disputes were settled by the fists. Police constables were few and far between. Nor were they any more keen than they sometimes are now to execute their function when circumstances sometimes rendered it necessary.

Another member of a School Board, also a large farmer, had occasion to cross a loch in a small rowing boat to attend the funeral of one of his shepherds. Accompanying him were other two men and the minister. On the return journey a heavy sea was running. Every moment the boat was in danger of being swamped. The situation became more and more perilous. When strenuous rowing was necessary one small man in a state of great trepidation suggested that his Reverence should pray. To this the farmer, noting the powerful build of the minister, replied, "Ach, no, Donald, you can do the praying and the minister can take an oar." At the same time he muttered *sotto voce* the Gaelic proverb, *"Is duilich ciall a thoirt do amadan"* (It's hard to give sense to a fool). He had evidently more faith in human muscle than in the supplication of aid from the Almighty. Some time after, when a friend referred to this miraculous escape from drowning, and his belief in the efficacy of prayer, the farmer cut short the conversation with, "Ach, yes; but I was very clever myself."

Chapter VIII

TEACHERS

'Poets are born, not made.' This trite proverb is essentially true of teachers. They vary in efficiency like the members of other professions. That some are unable to produce good results is their misfortune, not always their fault. But to one born to the profession without ills and harassments the work is congenial and stimulating.

I often thought it would be interesting to know the class from which certain teachers sprung. In the latter part of last century the industrial community supplied the bulk of them. Perhaps the comparatively meagre remuneration which then obtained accounted for this. A considerable number, however, were the daughters of clergymen and other professional men. One very able teacher of my acquaintance was the daughter of a baronet. Her sister was the wife of a distinguished headmaster of a large city school. When I visited the small school of the former she always made a point of inviting me to lunch at the completion of the examination. I can never forget my feelings as I sat in her little parlour at the meal, which was cooked and served by her estimable mother, who was as much entitled to be addressed as 'My Lady' as the wife of the noble lord on whose estate the school was situated. I gathered that the estates of the family had long passed into other hands; but the title had been handed down through many generations. As a fact the first baronet of the race was Chamberlain to Anne of Denmark, wife of James VI. of Scotland, in 1603. The baronetcy dated from 1631.

My long association with the teaching profession was fraught with much pleasure. I could always overlook idiosyncrasies and fads so long as they were harmless. Occasionally they afforded me much diversion. I remember one high-strung individual who was so obsessed with the necessity of preserving discipline in his school that after the pupils were dismissed, while I was engaging him in conversation, he suddenly whirled on his heel and shouted, "Whist! Whist!"

Another well-meaning dominie, when he heard his pupils talking, was continually shouting, "I will be wheeping you," directed to no one in particular. The utterance of this general threat through persistent reiteration entirely lost its effect, and the talking went on.

One teacher, who seldom associated with his fellow professionals, lived in a remote glen. He had a peculiar twist in his brain, which was generally more amusing than irritating. One year, when I scrutinised on the official form the names of the pupils who were being presented for examination, I noticed that his son, whom I knew by head-mark, figured under his 'middle' name to the omission of the surname. Thus John Smith Gunn appeared as John Smith. On my asking for an explanation he told me he never liked Gunn, and that he preferred Smith. Though I did not pursue discussion of the matter, I had in my thoughts that some relative may have brought disgrace on the Clan Gunn.

But I could not help laughing, and he too grinned when I suggested that he should make the youth a 'Gunsmith.' Needless to add, I insisted that the omission should be rectified at once and not repeated, otherwise the consequences might some day be serious. There is something after all in a name.

An old dominie in Argyll, for what reason he never would divulge, invariably used quills made from the feathers of his fowls, while his pupils wrote with ordinary pens. His own penmanship was exquisite, and compared favourably with what I have seen in old session books.

An excellent headmaster of my acquaintance affected a workmanlike appearance by teaching in his shirt-sleeves. Another I invariably found rigged out in trousers and jersey. When I first saw him I was forcibly reminded of a teacher whom I interviewed one broiling hot day in his wooden shanty of superimposed logs in the backwoods near Lake Huron in Canada. As I approached the open door seated in a light buggy I heard the sound of voices. The temptation to stop was irresistible. Entering, I explained what I was in justification of my intrusion. I discovered that his name was Fraser, and that he was a descendent of a Scottish family that had settled in the colony when it was still young. But what I can never forget was that the class was the fourth, and that each member held in his hand a reading book published by a well-known Edinburgh firm.

A teacher of the old parochial type invariably had his pupils singing as the Inspector entered his school. Nor did the song cease with the entrance of the emissary of My Lords. It had to be finished before he shook hands with him. It was generally 'Rule Britannia,' 'God save the Queen,' or some other ditty of patriotic sentiment, varied on at least one occasion by 'Wi' a hundred pipers an' a'.' I sometimes expected to hear 'See the Conquering Hero Comes' as I crossed the playground; but I never did, and I refrained from suggesting this for the sake of variety. To show that there was no ill-feeling when the pupils had made but an indifferent appearance, 'Will ye no' come back again' was sometimes sung with gusto as the Inspector quitted the school, where he knew only too well the sight of his back was more welcome than that of his face.

I was exceedingly sorry for one young lad in charge of a very small school in a group of houses near the mouth of an inlet on the Argyllshire coast. Failing to reach the ministry at which he aimed, he took to teaching where the possession of a teacher's certificate was not necessary. Shortly after I entered the school he drew my attention to a particular pupil in these words, "This boy is psychologically troubled with something on his brain. I believe myself it is some sort of sanguinary effusion due to consanguinity." Every time he addressed me he commenced with, "With your courtesy, sir," an expression as unusual as it was unnecessary. He had *'Dieu et mon droit'* written on every pupil's slate, perhaps as an antidote to the evil eye of the Inspector. Further, he had what I surmised from the character of the letters an inscription in Russian chalked on the wall. Poor lad, he was doing his best according to his lights; but the pupils were making no progress. The complaints I got from parents were fully justified. He shortly afterwards ceased to be a member of the teaching profession.

The first time I visited Cleish School in Kinross-shire the lines of Burns on the teacher of his day occurred to me: —

Here lie Willie M — hie's banes;
O Satan, when ye tak' him,
Gie him the schulin' o' your weans;
For clever deils he'll mak' 'em.

Aye! Aye! Willie must have been a tartar when he merited such a compliment from the National Bard.

The brawny female teacher with a manly voice was ever a source of interest. She only required the *toga virilis* to pass for a man. Some hefty Highland ladies could easily hold their own with the male sex in maintaining discipline. When the gentle, young female who taught a small school on the shore of a loch in Wester Ross demitted office, the parents sent a deputation to urge on the School Board that better discipline would be maintained, and consequently better results secured, were a man appointed to fill the vacancy. They also alleged that the dignity of their township would be enhanced through such an appointment. The Board, however, unanimously refused to accede to their request, chiefly because they knew that the salary paid to a female would be quite inadequate for the services of a male teacher. Now it happened that they had at that time in their employ in another similar school a female who stood six feet high, with shoulders half as broad. At the suggestion of the district Inspector, they transferred this well-proportioned Venus to the school by the loch, and they were greatly surprised that no complaints followed. The silence was explained one day when a native from the township happened to meet a friend, who put the usual question as to how they were getting on with their new teacher. With a shrug of his shoulders the former replied, "We wanted a man, but I will be thinking we have got one." It turned out that the discipline *had* improved, with every prospect of an increased grant at next inspection.

As an instance of what a determined female can effect, let me narrate the following. During the Great War the headmaster of a large school was called up for service. The Board, having had previous experience of her as a disciplinarian before she married, put a comparatively small but well-knit female in charge. She had one day chastised a big boy, who was a ringleader in rebellion, so effectively that after expelling him from the school his muscular mother, with sleeves rolled up, came to the door in a state of wrath and demanded to see the headmistress. The latter promptly appeared and asked what she wanted. "You have nearly killed my laddie," yelled the irate virago. "I know I have," said the teacher. "I almost wish I had." "Well, I have come to gie you a black e'e," said the mother. "All right," said the teacher, "just come out to the playground and we'll soon settle that." This invitation was very far from being expected. The determined attitude of the teacher took the breath from the aggrieved parent. Her anger vanished. On conditions her son was readmitted to the school, and ever after he was one of the best-behaved and obedient pupils in the senior department.

In the early years of the Education Act of 1872 teachers

whose salaries largely depended on the grant earned were more apt than they were latterly to correspond with the Inspector on school matters, often supplemented with details of domestic trials, sometimes, sad to say, quite fictitious. These were intended for sympathetic consideration. One teacher in particular, who taught a small school in a very remote corner of Ross-shire, was for years very persistent in writing letters to the Inspector about the time of inspection of his school. He was a man of some ability, but by no means a successful teacher. He was also lazy, and very far from being a total abstainer. On this account his poor wife, who never enjoyed good health, had not her sorrows to seek. Here is one of his typical epistles to the district inspector:

Dear Mr. P —,

Inexpressible by any form of speech is the anguish of my soul, and keen sorrow of heart when I beg to take the liberty of informing you that my beloved and comparatively young wife is to all appearance on her deathbed. Indeed her sufferings are so terrible that she is continually praying to God to take her away from this world of woes and sorrow. My present troubles have almost obliterated from my memory my late favourite boy who died last year so very suddenly. Oh! is God manifesting His displeasure at me for having been so much overwhelmed with unavailing grief at the loss of that fine, promising boy? In addition to my family calamities my mother-in-law died in my house on Thursday last. The funeral of the

old woman exposed me to more expenses than I am
able to bear. No form of speech can adequately
express the wretched state of both my mind and body.
My heart is all but completely broken. I am so
much overwhelmed with grief as to be hardly capable
of discharging my public duties, and I do feel that my
bodily health is a wreck. Would it be using too much
liberty to ask you for the loan of one pound? I must
candidly confess that it will be impossible for me to
repay it until I receive my share of the Government
Grant some time in Autumn.

I am, Dear Sir, Ever your faithful and
obedient servant, etc.

The letter is the product of a cute brain. In the epilogue
one pound, certainly not a large sum, is begged after the
Inspector is worked up to sympathy. Knowing as I did the
generous nature of the latter, I have no doubt he acceded to
the request, and probably added to the sum, even though he
had not the slightest hope of recovering the loan. He was
ever kind-hearted, with an open purse for a case of genuine
distress. Within my recollection he got at least one loan
repaid. It was during the distressful time referred to in the
chapter on Lewis. Gathering from a private talk with a
teacher's wife that there was no money in the house with
which to purchase bread for her large family, he at once
handed her five pounds without any stipulation as to
repayment. On my referring to this point he said quietly, "I
don't mind. She is an estimable woman and a good mother.

I am glad to be able to help her." As the event proved, she was what he proclaimed her, for some months later, as he was opening his correspondence, he showed me a five pound note which he found in a letter expressing warmest thanks and deepest gratitude for his kindness and timely assistance.

To be a prophet in one's own country is not always a handicap. Many teachers are natives of the district in which the school is situated. I was examining the highest class in a Uist school in reading, when I noticed that one boy had no book. On my asking for an explanation he at once replied, "Donald has it." Donald, I discovered, was the Christian name of the headmaster, who was a native of the place. To old and young he was known as Donald. Nor did this detract in the slightest degree from his efficiency as a teacher. He maintained excellent discipline, and commanded the highest respect from every member of the community.

The teacher of high-strung temperament was by no means a *rara avis* in the profession. The behaviour of the headmaster of a large town school once excited my risible faculties. The incident happened in the 'eighties of last century. The district Inspector was dealing with the infant department, where it was imperative that children over seven years of age should be in a class in keeping with their years. In a state of great excitement this master, doubtless anticipating my sympathy and assistance, rushed into my room, exclaiming, "He's looking at their teeth. This is shocking." Of course this criterion of a child's age is far from reliable, so I soothed his wounded feelings by assuring him that the Inspector was only joking, and that the dental scrutiny need not be taken seriously. I had a suspicion, however, that he left me unconvinced.

One teacher with a grievance was also a humorist. He explained the small number on his roll by what he described as the disgraceful conduct of the young men of the district, who persisted in remaining bachelors. However, he omitted to say anything about the young women, who were doubtless waiting till 'Barkis was willin'.'

Chapter IX

TEACHERS'
TRIALS

The trials and difficulties associated with teaching are both numerous and varied in character. Nor do they fall to the lot of one class or sex. Changing from one school to another, particularly in the Highlands and Islands, is often fraught with much anxiety due to uncertainty. I have seen the teacher, by no means young, trudging along on foot across the moors accompanied by her father, whom she was supporting in his old age. As I saw them making for their new home I was forcibly reminded of 'Nell and her Grandfather.' Oftener the teacher was the support of an aged mother. One unusual case I can never forget. The teacher's mother lived with her and looked after their little schoolhouse; but I could never address her as 'Mrs.' as she was still a spinster. Every time I visited the school I was impressed with the parent's comfortable surroundings, which, let us hope, were some measure of compensation for the scorn and mental agonies she probably endured when her child was born. As I wondered what would have been her fate had she not had that daughter, I am bound to admit I viewed with more charitableness than before the natural sins of commission of unthinking youth.

It was always painful to have to inspect the school of the female who suffered from neurasthenia. She was quite as ready to melt in tears over praise of her work as over censure, and one was always glad when the annual ordeal was past.

For various reasons teachers with physical defects are by no means common. When the defects become serious they generally retire from the profession. I may be pardoned for recording that I was amused when visiting one large school in Clackmannanshire for the first time to find the headmaster with only one hand, the first assistant lame, and the second with a wooden leg. But despite their defects the two assistants did credit to the profession, while the headmaster was a model of what one in his position should be.

In this same county a lady with a deformed hand taught needlework with exceptional success. Somehow the deformity seemed to foster a desire to excel in this particular branch.

The teacher of a small school in an island of the Inner Hebrides gradually lost his hearing. He was extremely energetic, and stuck to his profession. A better lip reader I never came across. I have heard him correct a pupil who pronounced 'attributed' with the accent on the wrong syllable. As a result of his defect the utterance of his pupils was exceptionally clear and accurate. He even professed 'singing.' More to gratify him than with any hope of hearing anything satisfactory, I selected one of the songs professed. It was amusing to see with what zeal he proceeded to use the pitchfork, though I am quite sure the vibrations were to him inaudible. As was to be expected, the singing was in a variety of keys, but the effort in such circumstances was commendable.

A female teacher of considerable ability assisted her sister, who was certificated, in the conduct of a small school in Argyllshire. And yet she was without arms. Well do I remember the shock I received when on my entering the school for the first time she approached me with two empty sleeves dangling from her shoulders. At the sight a lump rose to my throat though she met me with a smile. Strange to say, the specimens of manual work of various kinds executed by the pupils under her tuition were a special feature. She held the pen between her teeth when writing, and when she wished to draw my attention to something, she made use of a knee to bump me from behind.

In the days when the teacher's salary was largely dependent on the proficiency of his pupils, truancy and irregularity of attendance were particularly annoying. One teacher in Sutherlandshire explained the backwardness of his pupils as being due to absenteeism. Taking me to the door, he drew my attention to curls of smoke rising here and there from the valley beyond. These came from the bothy fires, by which at that moment boys in their teens were sitting instead of being present in school. If they were not learning to be intelligent citizens, they were certainly in training to be proficient smugglers.

Few people, and particularly those living in towns, have any conception of the trials of both teachers and pupils in some remote districts, where disagreeable atmospheric conditions prevail and roads are practically non-existent.

Take, for example, the district of Achosnich in Ardnamurchan. In my time the children had to cross miles of bogs and streams before they reached the school. Time and again I have regretted my not having a camera when on dismissing the pupils I beheld them clambering up the face of steep, wet rocks, the older ones assisting the younger to ascend. In addition to the possibility of accident from this mode of progression was the risk of being bitten by adders, which were, and still are, unusually numerous in this neighbourhood. But, although the pupils were generally barefooted, they were rarely bitten, probably because fear sharpened the power of observation, thus enabling them to shun them. After telling me how the crofters had lost a cow and a horse, besides some less valuable animals, through adder-bite, the teacher added that one afternoon as the little ones were being dismissed they returned to the classroom in a state of great trepidation. Investigating the cause, he discovered a beautiful specimen of an adder lying coiled up on the warm doorstep.

I have already referred to the remote group of islands called Monach, off the coast of North Uist. It may be of interest to some teachers to read of the hardships once endured by a young lady who happened to be the teacher here. Being non-certificated she had been studying hard in her spare time with a view to going to Glasgow to sit an examination for her parchment, as the teacher's certificate was called. In the latter half of last century these ordeals took place annually in December, a very unfortunate time for those who had to travel from islands and remote corners of the country. As bad luck would have it, the very day on which it was imperative that she should cross the sea to North Uist to enable her to catch the Glasgow steamer at Lochmaddy was exceptionally stormy. Huge waves with flying spray were rolling in from the broad Atlantic and breaking on the rocks. Besides, a fierce wind was blowing, and rain fell in torrents. Undaunted by the war of elements, and spurred on by the determination to reach the examination room, she pleaded with the male members of the little community to launch a boat; but although no more experienced and skilful boatmen could be found, one after the other, with his face turned to the riot of waves, merely shrugged his shoulders and shook his head. The poor girl was now in desperation. She had lived long enough in the island to know the folly of putting out an open boat in such a sea; but she resolved to run every risk in order to reach Glasgow in time. As a *dernier ressort* she approached the women-folks, who, out of sympathy and affection for her, actually urged their husbands to attempt the crossing. In the end the latter yielded to the appeal. The most suitable boat, such as was used for conveying peats from North Uist to the island, was launched. Into it scrambled two or three men and the teacher. A rag of a sail was hoisted with two reefs in, and with the eyes of the people left behind fixed on it, the boat dashed eastwards through the wild, green Atlantic rollers. But amongst the yawning billows progress was slow. Soon the sail was blown away, and the boat became almost waterlogged. Urging the teacher to lie down, the men allowed the boat to drift, the only thing they could do. After some hours it struck the shore of North Uist, fortunately not far from a hospitable manse. The kindly minister received the poor teacher, who was literally soaked to the skin. Her appearance, as he afterwards told me, was pitiful to behold. Kindness, supplemented by strong determination, helped to revive her, and, to make a long story short, she reached Glasgow in time for her examination, passed well, and in due course became a certificated teacher. But it was a terrible experience for a young girl. I never saw her again till over thirty years afterwards, when I came across her—a widow in charge of a small school in Argyll.

About a year after what I have described took place I happened to partake of lunch in the Established Church manse of Ferintosh in Ross-shire, then occupied by the Rev. Dr. Mackenzie, once Moderator of the Church of Scotland. Like his esteemed brother, the minister of Kingussie, I knew he was deeply interested in all matters connected with the Highlands and Islands. As I sat at table with him and his estimable lady, thinking that it would interest him, I recounted the foregoing stirring episode, but I soon regretted having done so. Though he remained silent during the narrative, his mind must have been very active, for, seemingly overcome by the thought of wives, out of sheer affection for the teacher, urging their husbands to risk their lives in her behalf, the old man quietly pulled a handkerchief from his pocket and wiped his eyes. The sight affected me, and to divert his thoughts I at once began to talk about a less disturbing Highland topic.

To find a young girl fresh from the Training College in charge of a small school far removed from the civilisation to which she had been accustomed, was apt to excite a sense of commiseration. Sometimes failing to get a situation nearer home, and disinclined to eat the bread of idleness, she had to accept an opening where the hermit life was apt to tell upon both nerves and constitution.

One young teacher accepted a post in an outlandish corner of a large island, where she found herself isolated from any congenial person of her own years with whom she could associate. When I first visited the school she had but recently entered upon her duties. The pupils numbered less than a dozen, and all lived some miles away. I don't think she had ever seen any of the parents. Yet she seemed quite happy and contented. On the occasion of my second visit to the school she struck me as being particularly alert, and inclined to take trifles too seriously. Candidly, I did not like her attitude, so I drew my own conclusions. The examination finished, she invited me into her house, where she lived alone, to partake of a cup of tea. This I was only too glad to accept, as I foresaw an opportunity of carrying out what I had in my mind. Whilst I waited in the semi-furnished room with not even the piano which one would have expected to find in such depressing surroundings, she busied herself in the kitchen, alternately whistling and singing. I realised that it was almost my duty, for I knew that she was an orphan, to lay before her a proposal that might be the means of perhaps saving her from herself. Accordingly, as I sipped the tea, I took the opportunity to suggest that it was time she were on the outlook for a post in a more populous place. She was startled, and naturally inquired if I was dissatisfied with her work. I assured her that no fault could be found with her teaching. In fact, I told her that it merited praise;

but I added that I considered her living all alone outwith the pale of congenial company was, in short, not good for her. She was obviously grieved. However, on second thoughts she agreed to my proposal that she should endeavour to obtain a situation somewhere on the mainland. To hearten her I gave her permission to use the Inspector's name for 'reference.' This she did, and shortly afterwards she was appointed to a good assistantship, which she filled till, like many more prepossessing females, she entered the bonds of matrimony.

Another comparatively young teacher, also in charge of an insular school, took her work so seriously that she became insane. To this I found out the harassment of unreasonable parents in some measure contributed. At the same time there may have been a hereditary predisposition to insanity. Her case was so bad that she had to be removed very hurriedly from her little schoolhouse to an asylum. There was ample evidence of this, for when I visited the school in charge of a temporary teacher shortly afterwards, having some time to spare before the arrival of my conveyance, I took a stroll round the house. What met my eyes was saddening in the extreme. There was the little garden, usually so tidy, overgrown with weeds. No blinds were drawn. Looking in, I saw on the window sill two pots of geraniums, all withered for want of water. Her nightdress was suspended on a chair by the bedside, just where it had been tossed when she rose for the last time. But what affected me most was the sight of a little cage suspended by a string from the top of the window. In it no bird was 'stirring nimbly.' Not 'the pressure of a finger' but starvation had done its work. The little warbler, that nobody had thought of caring for, lay dead. I turned away sick at heart. I had seen enough to depress me for the rest of that day.

The worries of teachers were sometimes due to defects in the structure of the school. The chimney that smoked was always a nuisance and source of irritation. One in particular occurs to me. It was in the small school of Boath in Ross-shire. When I entered the room one stormy winter day I found it seething with smoke. The School Board, I gathered, had done their best to improve the draught in the vent, but without success. The teacher, who bore his troubles philosophically, was a typical specimen of the cultured schoolmaster. A fine scholar, he taught classics with exceptional success. Of one of his pupils, a relative of his own, who at present fills a chair in Edinburgh University, the Inspector recorded in his Blue Book Report that in this small upland school he had come across the best Greek scholar in his district. I remember once examining two of his pupils orally in Latin. I was testing their knowledge of the idioms with which Melvin's versions bristled. For a few minutes the old man stood listening at my back. Then he took to walking up and down the floor. Finally he paused and whispered in my ear, "I see ye ken the sair bits."

Defective ventilation frequently added to the teacher's grievances. I must admit that I seldom found the expensive mechanical devices wholly effective. Curiously enough, in the Lewis schools the ventilation of the rooms was remarkably good. As the use of plaster for the ceilings was either unsuitable for the climate or too expensive, lining with very narrow pine laths was adopted. When these gradually shrank, cracks or openings occurred between every two laths. Through these the foul air gradually percolated, and found its way by the ordinary roof ventilators to the outside. Thus there was no perceptible draught even when the windows were opened, and the atmosphere of the classrooms was imperceptibly robbed of soporific effects.

Chapter X

TEACHERS' 'SINS'

Teachers, like members of other professions, are not without their faults and failings. At one time when the amount of the school grant, forming the major part of the teacher's salary, was to a large extent dependent on the attendance there was every inducement to falsify the registration. To check this, visits to the school without notice became specially necessary. Cases occurred, but they were happily rare, where two registers were kept, one showing the correct attendance, the other a concocted register from which the annual returns were made up. A case of this kind once caused an Inspector much annoyance. He had paid a surprise visit to a Highland school taught by a sedate-looking dominie of middle age. Going over the attendance for the day he discovered that four pupils who were absent were marked present. This was duly reported to the Department. Nothing more was heard of it till the end of the school year, when to verify some point the school register had to be sent to London. There it was found that the pupils whom the Inspector had reported as being absent on the occasion of his visit were actually marked absent on the register forwarded. The Inspector was naturally much disconcerted when asked for an explanation. He was quite certain that his finding was correct. He and I put our heads together, and concluded that two registers were being kept. Accordingly, it was arranged that I should pay a surprise visit to the school and endeavour to secure the other register. I set out, and by taking a devious course between the railway station and the school, I contrived to be on the school floor before the teacher could do anything to thwart the object of my visit had he been so inclined. He certainly appeared much taken aback when he saw me. After some casual remarks bearing on the small number of pupils present, I said I had as well examine the attendance register. This he promptly handed me as I seated myself at his desk. It was a rather bulky, well-thumbed volume, intended by the publisher to contain a record of two years' attendances at a small school. Turning back a few leaves as a preliminary, I observed date headings corresponding to those of the register sent to London. Accordingly, I at once concluded that I had before me the role which the Inspector had seen when he visited the school. As he surveyed my action I am certain that the teacher felt instinctively that he was caught, especially when I said that as the attendance appeared to be very intermittent, I was under the necessity of taking the register with me. He was a big, strong Highlander, and in a tussle I would probably have got the worst of it. Had he obtained possession of the register he could easily have burned it to hide his guilt. However, despite his strong remonstrances, I, greatly daring, bore off the volume, much to the relief of the Inspector concerned. The teacher, needless to say, paid the usual penalty of suspension for a year or two as a certified teacher.

When visiting a school without notice, one had to be very

careful before accusing a teacher of falsifying the registration. What sometimes led to suspicion was 'block marking.' That is to say, the marking for a whole week appeared to be in one uniform tone of ink, while the next would show a totally different shade. This would naturally indicate that the register was marked once a week instead of twice a day according to the statutory regulations. A case occurred in a very remote Hebridean island, where I afterwards thought the teacher had been unjustly punished for 'block-marking.' And here I may add that in these far-off places, where the teacher's salary was quite inadequate to meet the needs of a family, there was great temptation to defraud. This man's certificate was cancelled for one year; but, considering his domestic circumstances, the School Board allowed him to continue teaching, provided he paid a sum equivalent to the grant lost through his wrong-doing. When the school was visited in the following year the Inspector was more than surprised to note that the registration presented the same block-marked appearance. Drawing the teacher's attention to this he asked for an explanation. The man, who from his bearing always looked incapable of acting dishonestly, quietly remarked, "I have been thinking over it, and I am now certain that it is the ink I use that's to blame. I use Duckett's ink, which I get in cake form for convenience. Every other week, when I make up a new supply, it is apt to effect a different shade from the last, so the markings for a week would all appear to be done at one time." The Inspector accepted the explanation without remark; but I know he left that school with an uncomfortable feeling that the teacher had been unfairly sacrificed on the altar of Duckett's ink.

An amusing case of careless registration occurred in a

small school in the far north. It was done through sheer laziness, and with no intention of defraud. At a surprise visit the Inspector found that the teacher had neglected to make attendance entries of any kind in his register for a whole month. For various reasons, after rating him soundly and pointing out the serious consequences which such an offence entailed, the Inspector let him off, as the law has it, 'with an admonition.' Of course, he admitted his guilt, and earnestly promised to be more careful in future. Nothing more was said of the affair. Some time later I happened to be passing his school, so I looked in to see how the registration was progressing. *Horresco referens!* I found that he had filled in the attendances of his pupils for a month ahead. There is a limit to condonation. The sequel was that he wisely took to the grocery trade in a small town not far from his school. At it, I believe, he did remarkably well; but I should be surprised if he ever kept any books recording commercial transactions from which an annual balance sheet could be constructed.

One teacher in a remote corner of western Inverness-shire boasted to his confreres that no Inspector could visit him unawares. The fact was that some official of his acquaintance was bribed to send him due warning when an Inspector was travelling westwards by the Skye railway. I undertook to upset his confidence in immunity from a surprise visit. To effect my purpose, instead of booking to Strome Ferry, the terminus nearest to his school, I took a ticket for Portree in Skye, whence I caught a steamer that landed me within little more than a mile of his school. His face was worth photographing when he saw me standing on the schoolroom floor. He blurted out, "You have caught me; but tell me how

you managed it, for you did not come off at Strome Ferry."
However, I kept my secret to myself, and I believe he never
did find out how I managed to surprise him. I am pleased to
record that I found nothing flagrantly wrong with the registration, and certainly nothing which justified his boast of
safety from an inspectorial raid.

Even the most trustworthy teachers were not
enamoured of visits without notice. They alleged that they
savoured of espionage. Nor did a teacher scruple to let his
neighbour know when the Inspector was on the wing. Once,
when doing a round of visits in order to check the registration and adherence to the time-tables, I overtook a strong,
barefooted boy hurrying along for all he was worth in the
same direction as myself. Thinking that he was concerned in
some serious matter where expedition was necessary, I bade
my driver halt to give him a lift. On my asking where he was
going, he informed me that he was sent as fast as he could to
tell Mr. — (the teacher of the neighbouring school) that he
might look out for the Inspector at any minute. More amused
than angry, I kept him on the box seat till I reached the
school, when I handed him a shilling for being a good lad in
having carried out his master's instructions. I overheard him
deliver his message as I entered, to find that the registration
of the forenoon's attendances had been omitted. I did wish
that I had been a listener to the discussion of the incident
when the two dominies had their tête-à-tête that evening, in
all likelihood over a much needed potation.

When one found a teacher of brilliant attainments and
possessing a University degree in charge of a small school in
some remote Highland glen or island, it was almost safe to

conclude that he had seen better days, and that spirituous liquor had led to his downfall. I have oftener than once examined the school of a teacher in a state of intoxication. But I must admit I had a measure of sympathy for the high-strung dominie who, in the days of the cast-iron code, finding the examination getting on his nerves, made repeated visits to his house for consolation from his better half and a potent beverage to sustain him till the ordeal was concluded. Unfortunately the aroma pervading the schoolroom induced the pupils to be more interested in the teacher than in the Inspector. By the end of the day his articulation was so incoherent that one gave no offence by departing without the usual formality of shaking hands.

The teacher who had the misfortune to commit a *faux pas* had almost invariably to leave the district. Sometimes he went abroad. Oftener he found a situation in some far-off region, where investigation as to his previous career was not considered necessary. One sprightly young man, an excellent teacher, got into trouble in a mainland school. Consequently he disappeared, nobody knew where. Years after, on a warm summer day, I happened to be sent to examine a school in a very remote island. Wiping the perspiration from my brow, for I had walked a few miles, I was met at the gate by this same teacher. He appeared too much taken aback to be able to utter the usual salutation of pleasure at seeing the Inspector. I noted his hesitancy, and only too mindful of his past career, I blurted out, "Be sure your sins will find you out." He seemed relieved when I patted him on the back, as I assured him he had nothing to fear, provided he maintained his reputation as a capable teacher. At the conclusion of a successful examination I parted from him full of sympathy for those who have not the power to resist the temptations that humanity in every sphere is subjected to.

I frequently visited the school of a stolid-looking Highlander, who, not being a successful teacher, showed his deep-rooted antipathy to the cast-iron code by writing objectionable entries in his log book. One wintry day when I visited his school without notice, I found that the registers should have been marked an hour before I arrived. His explanation was that the clock having stopped the time for religious instruction had been prolonged. And, indeed, this seemed justifiable, for I found the senior pupils vieing with one another as to who would shout loudest in their effort to commit to memory the Second Commandment, while he stalked about inflicting corporal punishment with a pair of taws on those who he considered were not giving sufficient attention to the task. Here is a specimen of an entry in his log book: "Our school year has come to an end to-day. Well, whatever the results may be, we can honestly affirm that we have worked. The Hebrews are said to have had hard times under their Egyptian taskmasters; but with what feelings, it may be asked, would they have regarded their lot had they been compelled to work under the revised code?" Evidently the code for the year had prescribed some additional work which he found irksome. The following is another entry which struck me as being clever: "The pupils are now struggling amid the shoals and quicksands of Reduction." But really he was not to be taken too seriously. I always got on well with him, and he was deservedly popular in the district.

Once upon a time cases occurred where bribing the

Inspector was attempted. It invariably did not meet with success. As two of us were once leaving a school in the Hebrides the teacher's wife insisted on depositing a full-grown turkey in our wagonette. We knew only too well the purpose of the gift, for the pupils had made a somewhat poor appearance. The turkey was declined with thanks as my companion muttered, *Timeo Danaos et dona ferentes*.

Only one teacher ever attempted to extort from me money which he had no intention of repaying. He was a foreigner, and taught modern languages in an academy. To effect his purpose he sent me a letter containing a cock-and-bull story setting forth that he was a shareholder in a large private school in England, and that to meet an urgent and unexpected call he required a loan of twenty pounds. Enclosed in the letter was a blank cheque signed, which I was to present at his bank four months hence, after inserting twenty-five pounds in it. The extra five pounds were to be my reward of my generosity. But I did not rise to the occasion. I had previously heard rumours of his being in financial difficulties. One month after he sent me the cheque he suddenly departed from the district. Some years later I read in a newspaper that he had committed suicide in a Paris hotel. All the same, he was a capable teacher and kind-hearted. But debt proved his undoing, as it has done in the case of many an able teacher.

In the small island of Grimisay, off the north coast of Benbecula, the teacher in my time had an intense dislike to spitting. As it happened, he was of a religious turn, and for the benefit of the little community wherein his lot was cast, he considered it his duty to conduct weekly prayer meetings in the school. I was told, and knowing him as I did I could well believe it, that one evening while he was engaged in prayer he heard repeated expectorations on the floor. Having frequently at secular meetings expressed his objection to what he was wont to describe as pools the size of the continent of Europe, his thoughts were soon more concentrated on the spitting than on the prayer. His wrath rose in proportion to the persistence of the expectoration. Forgetting that 'to be in anger is impiety,' he suddenly stopped, and, characterising the assembly as a pack of pigs, ordered the whole lot of them to the door. But after all it was a case of *hominem non odi sed ejus vitia*. He commanded the respect of the natives, the majority of whom sympathised with him in his sanitary punctiliousness.

A teacher, who found his profession somewhat trying, had great belief in the efficacy of prayer. Every morning he was wont to supplicate the Almighty in these words, "And now, Lord, harden my heart and strengthen my arm for the duties of the day!" Perhaps his love for his pupils would account for his liberal administration of chastisement.

As an illustration of the discomfiture of a teacher of the old school when the members of the Presbytery came annually to examine his classes, I may be excused for narrating the following anecdote, which for all I know may be an oft-told tale. It was in the days before the passing of the Education Act of 1872, when instruction in religious knowledge formed an important item of the school curriculum. This teacher was afflicted with laziness, so to save himself trouble he devised a plan to bluff the ministers. The younger pupils had to commit to memory the answers to the questions in what was called *The Mother's Catechism*, as distinct from *The Shorter Catechism*. The first question was, 'Who made you?'—the answer being 'God'; the second, 'Who is it that redeems you?'—answer, 'The Holy Ghost;' and so on. Instead of insisting that each child should commit to memory the answers to all the questions, he made each memorise the answer to one particular question, and so arranged the class that when drawn up for examination the sequence of questions and answers would be complete. Unfortunately, on one occasion the child who had to answer the first question was not in his place. Accordingly, the second one was asked, 'Who made you?' He hesitated for a moment, and, suppressing the usual confident tone of the boy who answers with decision, looking up into the interrogator's face, he whispered naïvely, "Please, sir, the laddie that God made has just gane oot to spue." History is silent as to the sequel, but doubtless the teacher, who almost invariably formed one of the guests at the subsequent ministerial banquet, would not be in a frame of mind to enjoy the laughter which the rehearsal of the incident for the benefit of the hostess and her lady friends was sure to have evoked.

Chapter XI

LEWIS

The island of Lewis, the well-known 'Eilean-an-fhraoich,' recently owned by Lord Leverhulme, presented so many peculiar features in the 'eighties of last century, when I visited it officially, that it merits a chapter to itself. It is joined to Harris at its southern end, and except for a series of patchy strips of cultivable land by the seaboard, where the townships are situated, it consists for the most part of great melancholy stretches of heather-covered moors and peaty bogland, scattered over which are innumerable lochs. Except in Uig, on the far west side, where Mealasbhal rises to 1730 feet in height, the island is comparatively flat. Stornoway, with its fine modern castle, is a busy seaport, and possesses a flourishing secondary school.

When thinking of Lewis one cannot get away from the sea. On a summer evening, when 'the western wave is all aflame,' a sight that will never leave the memory is that of a full-rigged ship, with every stitch of canvas set, creeping along in a favourable breeze off the Flannan Isles on the far-stretching Atlantic. She is probably bound for Dundee with a cargo of jute from Calcutta. It is a wonderful sight. No steamer can approach it in majesty. These isles are memorable for the tragic incident so beautifully rendered in verse by Rupert Brooke. On one of them stands a lonely lighthouse. One day a passing steamer brought news to Stornoway that the lights were seen burning by day. The matter was at once investigated, when it was found that the lighthouse keepers had disappeared. The mystery is still unsolved, though various conjectures have been advanced in explanation.

The farmer in Lewis who rented the rich grazing on the isles told me he sometimes missed sheep and found others lame through gunshot wounds. These, he concluded, were inflicted by sailors of passing ships, who, when their vessel was becalmed, seized the opportunity to land for a supply of fresh mutton.

The population outside Stornoway is for the most part confined to the coast. In those years the bulk of the people were engaged in crofting and fishing. The real harvest of Lewis was, and probably still is, the harvest of the sea. A poor season's fishing meant more distress than the failure of the potato crop, on which much reliance was placed, for so long as the native had his *sgadan agus buntàta* (herring and potatoes) for dinner he never grumbled. As a rule the women tilled the lazy beds, as the patches of collected soil were called, and left to the men, who were essentially *travailleurs de la mer*, to concern themselves about the fishing. Both sexes, however, took part in cutting peats, their sole supply of fuel, which could be had in abundance and of excellent quality. These the women bore to the townships in creels. Though the inhabitants might be considered industrious, they were very rarely in what might be called affluent circumstances. As Dr. Johnson wrote of Robert Levett:

The modest wants of every day,
The toil of every day supplied.

When I was in the way of visiting Lewis the Education Act was in full swing, and the education of the children was a burning topic all over the island. The new schools, all of the same style of architecture, chiefly consisted of one long room, with one or two classrooms annexed, in which the younger pupils were taught by a pupil teacher or certificated female assistant.

At that time the enforcement of the Act was handicapped through English-speaking teachers having to deal with children whose mother tongue was Gaelic. Well-trained Celtic teachers were scarce. All of them did yeoman service in the face of most discouraging circumstances. In a majority of cases their remuneration depended on the grant earned. Sad to say, it was sometimes barely sufficient to provide the necessaries of life. The bulk of the natives could not be described as of cleanly habits. The children often wore their scanty clothing till it was literally in rags. Almost all were barefooted in both summer and winter. It was customary to see women crossing the moors barefooted, but a man was rarely seen without boots on his feet. To save her husband the trouble of taking them off, when a stream had to be forded his wife transported him in her creel. Seeing this, I often wished that the *ithish* or straw rope across her breast would snap and let the unmanly burden drop into the water.

Let me now describe a Lewis crofter's home, or 'black house,' as it was appropriately called at least half a century ago. It consisted of two tiers of dry stone walls, with a padding of earth between them. On the top of the four feet thick walls grass generally grew, sometimes so profusely that I have seen a woman hoisting a lamb to feed on it. The roof consisted of rough cabers covered with a thick layer of straw held down by ropes or rapes of twisted heather, with big terminal stones to keep it from being blown off. Rarely was any sort of chimney seen by which the thick peat smoke could make its exit. As a rule there was a hole near the bottom of the thatch for the convenience of the poultry. The smoke from the peat fire in the middle of the floor percolated through the thatch, which in time became laden with a good deposit of soot. Annually the thatch was carefully stripped off by the men and carried in creels by the women to the potato patches, where it was laid alongside the drills for the nourishment of the sprouting tubers. The Lewis crofter would rather endure cold than part with his soot. The Gaelic proverb bears this out: *Is fhearr an toit na' ghaoth tuath* (The smoke is better than the north wind).

At different ends of these black houses the family and the cattle, generally separated by a low wall, shared the accommodation. In such circumstances sanitation and cleanliness could not be expected. To remove the manure at a certain time of the year the end wall of the house had to be taken down. It was then that scarlet fever became prevalent, and sometimes carried off whole families. But what disgusted the Inspector most was the occasional verminous condition of the children. I have seen a pretty little girl so tormented that in the midst of her reading she tossed the book on the floor and vigorously scratched herself, the while eyeing first me and then her teacher with a troubled expression of uncertainty as to how this departure from good behaviour would be received.

Sometimes the animals also made themselves comfortable in the fire end of the house. One day after the examination of a school on the west side I visited a crofter's house across the road. When I opened the door the volume of smoke almost blinded me. This explained the prevalence of opthalmia amongst the children. Entering, I could just distinguish in the distance the subdued glow of a peat fire in the middle of the floor. I made in that direction, and as I neared it I saw beyond the fire a girl that had just arrived home from the school. When I drew near her she stepped back over some object at her feet. This I was amused to discover was a full-grown pig, which was lying comfortably by the side of the fire at her heels.

Here I may mention that I have heard it said that a stranger from the south can only gaze in wonder at these black houses resembling African kraals. I was forcibly reminded of the state of matters in Lewis half a century ago when I recently read the following account of the Bantu tribe in South Africa: 'The primitive dwellings have no chimney, though a fire is often lit, and a lot of cooking done in the centre of the floor. When a fire is set agoing the smoke simply fills the house and escapes by the doorway if the door happens to be open. It is needless to say that eye trouble is very common among the Bantu people.... In some parts along with sleeping humanity may be found dogs, cats, fowls and pigs. ...The women are the beasts of burden. They toil in the fields; they fetch the water,' etc., etc. I leave the reader to make comments.

One fine summer evening as two of us were passing a black house while returning from a distant school we saw a girl, a dog, a pig and a calf with noses pointing to the door, ready to dart inside as soon as it was opened. The girl's finger was on the latch. The temptation to bet as to what would be first inside was irresistible. I put my stake on the dog and lost. Immediately the door was opened the pig first crossed the threshold.

About the year 1886 people at the Butt of Lewis were stirred by a tragedy which occurred at the uninhabited island of North Rona, lying about thirty miles to the northward. Three or four men from Ness had gone out there to kill seals and edible aquatic birds. When they failed to return at the appointed date their relatives became alarmed. A boatload of men set out to investigate. They found them all dead. I always regretted not accepting the piece of wood which the Fiscal offered me after his official visit to the island. On its edge were the notches, including a deeper one to indicate Sabbath, which told the number of days they had been on the island before the last man died.

Inspection of the evening classes every winter was always trying. The stormy Minch had to be crossed, and woe betide the Inspector if he happened to be a bad sailor. I often recall my arrival at Stornoway pier, lit up by a few sickly-looking lamps, the intense darkness at that late hour, the piercing cold, the driving rain or sleet, and the walk to my lodging with my heavy ulster buttoned close up to my chin. The old landlady, who had for an hour or more been watching for the light of the steamer in the bay, as she opened the door, invariably met me with a warm welcome in Gaelic. And what could be more cheering than the sight of a glowing peat fire, the tea set, and the glorious fresh herring reeking on the table? The appetite appeased, I betook myself to bed in the warm garret. Then followed sleep ever so sound, with the turmoil of winds and waves still ringing in my ears.

The grants for conducting these classes were given entirely to the teachers, who did their utmost to induce the young folks of both sexes to come forward for instruction for two or three evenings each week during the winter months. To secure grants the Inspector had to visit the classes and examine the pupils individually in the subjects professed.

It took some courage to face the elements, even in a closed carriage, for the twenty-five mile drive to the Butt of Lewis. Motor cars were unheard of in those days. And be it noted the roads were narrow and badly kept, while the wide, stretching moors were swept with biting winds frequently laden with sleet or snow. Then the darkness, which the feeble candle lights on each side of the box seat almost failed to penetrate, was sometimes terrifying. The long, cold, monotonous drives would often have been depressing had I not devised a way of making the time pass quickly and enjoyably. On leaving a school I bade the driver halt at the first peat stack he came to on the roadside. Jumping out, by the aid of one of the carriage lamps, I selected as large a peat as I could lay hands on. This I took into the carriage. I next cut a hole in the centre big enough to hold the end of a candle stump. Splutter as it might while the conveyance jolted slowly along, the grease did no damage to the cushioned seat. Then on a plaid stretched across our knees my chief and I beguiled the weary hours playing a game of cards, popularly known as 'snap,' till we reached Stornoway. The gambling, which was on the smallest scale, in our estimation was never more excusable. We played to pass the time, not for the love of the filthy lucre. The moisture that naturally gathered on the inside of the windows kept any natives who might have been abroad at that late hour from seeing our occupation as we jogged along through township after township.

Only once during a snowstorm, when the moorland road near the Butt was quite obliterated, did we have our game suddenly interrupted by the carriage and horses tumbling into a deep ditch. Though 'safety first' was our native driver's motto, he could not have avoided this accident. However, we succeeded in scrambling out without injury, and the soft, deep snow prevented damage to our equipage.

One very dark, stormy night I was almost persuaded not to visit the evening class conducted in Bragar School. But I was anxious to secure a grant for the poor teacher, which rendered a visit from the Inspector imperative. Accordingly, despite what I knew was facing me, I set out in drenching rain in a dogcart from Barvas Inn. A stream that was in heavy flood had to be forded. When the water was well up my legs, and almost over the horse's back, I was fain to think that my solicitude for the benefit of my fellow-men had about reached its limit. However, I succeeded in winning through all right, executed my task, and regained the inn in safety.

Seeing me so often in Lewis, the natives, and particularly the young generation, treated me with much familiarity till troubles to which I shall refer later tended to alter matters. From them I sometimes received interesting small gifts. On one occasion, however, the proffered gift had for sanitary reasons to be declined. I had spent an afternoon alone fishing on a distant loch. As the evening closed in I reeled up, and made a bee-line across the heathery moor towards the public road. On the way I happened upon a shieling, or *airigh*, as it is called in Gaelic, perched upon a rising ground. A shieling is a hut consisting of turf walls roofed over with a few cabers covered with a liberal coating of long heather. It is erected at a considerable distance from the township, and hence it is sometimes referred to as the 'lone shieling.' Round it the cattle graze, while in it two or three young women take up their abode temporarily. When not herding and milking the cows they spend their time making butter and cheese. They also by means of the distaff spin worsted to be used in making home-made tweeds in the winter months. The life is exceedingly monotonous, but they get used to it at a very early age. As I approached the shieling referred to, I saw two or three girls well on in their teens. I knew from their laughter that they recognised me, for they had often seen me in school. Noticing me wiping the perspiration from my brow, the oldest one offered me a drink of milk. When I expressed acceptance she forthwith produced from the interior of the hut a 'craggan.' This is a globe-shaped clay vessel of home manufacture peculiar to Lewis. It appeared to be about half-full of milk, which, to judge from the general appearance of the vessel, was by no means inviting. But what disgusted me was that before handing it to me she inserted her forefinger in the liquid and gave it a circular motion, intended, no doubt, to mix the thick cream with the milk. This was enough. I suddenly discovered that milk so rich in cream might not agree with my stomach in my heated state. I expressed a preference for water, which was sullenly forthcoming, and, bidding them *oidche mhath!* (good evening) proceeded on my journey.

That night I passed two primitive mills for grinding oats. As I was alone I had leisure to examine one of them. It consisted of a hut built over a stream, and was common property. The rushing water dashing against flanges fixed to a central upright piece of wood or tree trunk causes it to revolve. A stone is attached to the top end in the hut. As the trunk revolves this rubs on a similar flat, stationary stone underneath it. The oats, in a bag suspended above, find their way into a hole in the middle of the revolving stone. A short stick, having one end attached to the bag and the other rubbing on the revolving stone, causes a quivering motion, which ensures that there is a constant trickle of grain into the central aperture. After it is ground it oozes out round the edges. It is then collected in the form of coarse meal. The whole contrivance is really the ancient quern driven by a stream. I have seen a series of these primitive mills on one stream in Valtos, on the west side of the island. They may be there to this day.

The foregoing has been written the more easily to enable the reader to grasp what follows. Education in Lewis had been proceeding satisfactorily from the passing of the Act of 1872 till about the middle of the 'eighties, when a land agitation commenced among the crofter population in the various townships, but particularly in those adjacent to the farms of which strangers from the mainland were tacksmen. Disturbances in a community react on the children. The poverty of the people, who begrudged the best parts of the islands given over to these incomers, spurred them on to rebellion and open hostility to the officials administering the estate. To make matters worse agitators appeared on the scene. One was the schoolmaster of Balallan, who was subsequently known by this name. The result was that law-breaking became the order of the day. Hefty young men invaded the farm lands, threw down fences, and proceeded to plant potatoes, at the same time grazing their cattle on grass much richer than that growing on the portions allotted to them as common pasture. This lawlessness had a baneful effect on the education of the children. Starvation prevailed. Hungry, half-naked pupils were herded to the schools by the harassed compulsory officers, whose task was an invidious one. The cry of distress echoed over the land. It soon reached Glasgow, where dwelt plenty of sympathetic Highlanders and relatives of the crofters. Forthwith, to relieve the distress, from that quarter sacks of oatmeal, with innumerable tins of syrup and treacle, were hurried to Stornoway and distributed amongst the townships for the feeding of the children. The food had to be cooked and served in school. Here originated the trouble for both teachers and Inspectors. Porridge freely bespattered on desks was bad enough; but when flimsy copy-books and examination papers adhered to spilt treacle irritation reached its extremity. Still, the children were hungry, so one had just to thole and make the best of a trying situation. It was in the school at Cross, near the Butt, where I witnessed a state of matters that almost brought tears to my eyes. It was a beautiful, sunny day, with no trace of cloud above the sparkling waters of the heaving Atlantic stretching far away to the western horizon. My chief and I, after covering the twenty-two miles from Stornoway, arrived at the school about two o'clock in the afternoon. As the examination proceeded I noticed that every now and then several of the children were vomiting water. Becoming alarmed lest this might be evidence of some incipient epidemic, I consulted the teacher. He simply shook his head, as with a doleful countenance he assured me that the children had had nothing to eat since they left their beds, and that to allay the pangs of hunger they had been drinking water to excess all the forenoon. He knew that there was practically no food in the homes. I afterwards learned to my horror that any money there was had gone on the previous Sunday to swell the sustentation fund contributed by members of the local Free Church. The feeding of the children was evidently a secondary matter compared with the call of religion. And yet children in such deplorable circumstances had to be taught and examined at the end of the school year.

In course of time matters went from bad to worse. Law-breaking was steadily on the increase. The Government had to step in. Two gunboats, the *Seahorse* and the *Bellisle*, having on board armed marines, were despatched to Stornoway. At that time the young men of Lewis were reputed to consti-tute the finest body of naval reserves in the United

Kingdom. It was therefore not to be wondered at that both the local Sheriff and Fiscal shuddered to contemplate what might eventuate should these hefty, trained Hebrideans and the red-coated marines come to grips. The handling of the situation called for the utmost tact. Luckily, these two officials were capable of exercising it.

Never was cool judgement and self-restraint more called for than during an ugly episode at Knock, a few miles from Stornoway. Here the crofters were committing serious depredations on an adjoining farm. The marines were sent for. Accompanying them were both the Sheriff and Depute Fiscal, who himself was an officer in the militia. When they were drawn up in battle array with loaded rifles and fixed bayonets, facing a defiant crowd, the tension, as the Fiscal told me, was appalling. The crofters showered stones on the soldiers, while their womenfolk carried lapfuls for this purpose from the adjacent beach. The marines could with difficulty be restrained, but still the Sheriff refused to grant the necessary permission to open fire. And, indeed, it was doubtless well he adopted this attitude, for it would almost to a certainty have followed that the trained crofter assailants, maddened by the inevitable wounding and perhaps death of companions, would have rushed upon the soldiers, with the result that one of the saddest and greatest tragedies in the history of the Highlands would have had to be recorded.

While the warships were lying at anchor in the bay the annual inspection of the schools was being overtaken, often at much inconvenience due to the unsettled state of the populace. This was imperative to secure grants for the poor teachers, whose coffers were being badly depleted chiefly through irregularity of attendance resulting from the indifference of parents, who had other things to think about than the education of their children.

The commanders of these vessels, as well as the crews, so far from civilisation, soon began to get weary of the monotony of inactivity. With the captain of the *Seahorse* my chief struck up an acquaintance, which resulted in an arrangement being concluded between the War Office and the Education Department, whereby we were to get the use of the ship to enable us to inspect four schools lying on the east coast, south of Stornoway. This promised to be an interesting outing for all concerned. As there was no lack of accommodation, invitations to accompany us were extended to all our friends, and about eight o'clock one fine morning the warship's anchors were weighed. The schools were small, situated inland near the head of narrow inlets. But the commander passed an anxious time. The man swinging the lead to ascertain the depth of water as we crept forward had his work cut out for him. The sound of the great siren, echoing amongst the rocks intimating our approach, naturally alarmed the natives. We saw them scurrying in all directions, probably to give timely warning to neighbours that the townships were on the verge of bombardment. On second thoughts, however, they no doubt realised that this was only a new way of visiting the schools, of which the teachers had due intimation. The inspections being completed, everybody enjoyed the homeward journey. This was surely the only occasion on which a warship was ever used for the inspection of public schools.

I often thought, however, that this incident did not make for friendly feelings between the crofters and the inspectorate. Subsequent events almost confirmed me in this surmise. As the seizure of land and destruction of property constituted the main feature of the prevailing lawlessness, the local factor, estimable man, became deeply involved. Unfortunately he and my chief were close friends. From being seen so often in each other's company the natives naturally concluded that even the Inspector did not bear any particular good-will towards them. Then, my chief and I being so much associated with one another, I am afraid I to some extent came into the same hostile category. One incident, which might have had serious consequences, showed this. On the homeward journey from a school on the east side of the island our wagonette and pair had to cross a wooden bridge, where a stream debouched into the sea. The bridge consisted of a series of long planks like railway sleepers laid side by side. There was no parapet. In course of years through constant traffic and stress of weather the planks had become so worn and decayed that gaping holes between them were numerous. As we moved cautiously on to the bridge, a large spade used for cutting peats was suddenly thrust upwards through one of the openings right in front of the horses. Instantly they reared and backed. The driver, no friend of the crofters, for they had ere this invaded his father's farm, at once tossed the reins to my companion. Knowing that the culprit must still be in concealment under the bridge, he bade me go down one side while he went down the other. There we discovered two young crofter lads. It was a time for deeds, not words.

We were not long in taking the law into our own hands. Without compunction we taught the victims of our wrath a lesson which they would not soon forget.

But winter came, when we once more visited the island for the examination of the evening classes. This proved the most trying time of all, because the journeys had to be made under cover of darkness. But except for two rather exciting incidents the work was quietly overtaken.

We had finished the examination of the classes held in Carloway School, on the far west side, and were returning to Stornoway in the usual closed carriage. The road wound round the face of a hill, with a steep slope down to a loch on one side. There was no protecting wall of any kind. It was a frosty night, and the water on the loch was frozen. As the horses came round a sharp bend they were suddenly confronted with a sheet of white ice standing erect right in the middle of the road. Had the driver not been keeping a very careful lookout, or the horses been high-spirited, a tragedy might have happened. The carriage might have been precipitated down the incline into the loch. No doubt this was what was intended by the miscreants, who, however, were never found out. Detection, where the bulk of the people were united against a common enemy, was practically hopeless. We afterwards learned from a reliable source that a rumour had got abroad that the factor was in the carriage along with the Inspector. This, of course, was not the case. The attack was no doubt meant for him. The Inspector had just to take his chance of escaping scatheless. In these days the spirit of mischief seemed to be the ascendant. Religion, despite the usual churchgoing and the preaching of all the horrors of eternal retribution for evildoers, was of no avail to check it. I have witnessed men returning from church breaking down the farmer's fences.

To myself a more exciting experience befell one very dark winter night. An evening school about eight miles from Stornoway was taught by a teacher who had a large family. I knew he was in need of money, and that it was essential that he should get a grant for his evening classes. At the same time the locality in which the school was situated was seething with lawlessness. The Depute Fiscal, who was also Clerk of the School Board, knowing that I intended to visit the classes, came to me before I set out and explained the risk I was running in going near the neighbourhood at night. As he said, after what had happened on the Carloway road, anything might occur to me or any other official owing to the highly inflamed state of the community. At that time the marines were encamped in and around the school playground. However, in spite of his urging me not to go, as I had already ordered a dogcart, I was determined to make the attempt. But his picture of the situation was so gloomy that I must confess my nerves almost got the better of me. No doubt noticing from my attitude that I was not quite at ease mentally, he laughingly suggested my going armed, in case I should be exposed to rough usage. Although I hardly conceived it possible that this was at all likely, on the spur of the moment I took his suggestion in all seriousness. Without the least intention of using it, I put a loaded revolver in my pocket, and, taking a seat beside the driver, set out into the darkness. I may explain that I happened to have the weapon in my possession, having purchased it some years before for self-protection when on a holiday in Canada and the United States. Otherwise I should have been without it. But, after all, these were troublous and uncertain times, and anything which might inspire confidence was welcome. As might be expected, where dangerous turns had to be negotiated, we proceeded cautiously, with both eyes and ears open for the least indication of danger. But, just as I anticipated, nothing untoward occurred. Arrived at the school gate, I well remember my sensations when I detected the white military tents of the marines illumined by the paraffin lamps in the school windows. At the gate, by official orders, two policemen were waiting to guard the conveyance while I was in the school, lest some ill-conditioned wretch might seize the opportunity under cover of darkness to damage the harness. Ere this the bulk of the young lads forming the class had realised that the purpose of my visit was for the benefit of the teacher, to whom they bore no ill-will, since he wisely abstained from interfering in matters connected with the crofter agitation, which he neither countenanced nor condemned. This of itself was sufficient to save me from any form of molestation, especially as I was travelling alone. The examination passed off satisfactorily, much to the relief of the teacher as well as myself. With a few jokes, as I buttoned up my ulster, I took my departure, leaving everybody in good humour. I daresay I am safe in saying that no Inspector of Schools in this or any other country for that matter, ever had the experience, unnecessary though the event proved, of examining an evening school with a loaded revolver in his pocket.

During a visit to Lewis in the previous summer I saw an amusing incident while I was staying a night at Galson, a large sheep farm on the west coast, where the Atlantic waves breaking on the rocks below the farmhouse were always a source of interest. The crofters in the neighbouring township had been very troublesome. Two of the more reckless of them, asserting that since they were natives they had more right to the grazing on Galson than the tacksman, broke down a wooden fence and allowed their horses to roam at will on the forbidden pasture. The farmer, with the aid of a manservant, promptly caught and imprisoned the vagrants in a cowshed. Here he had kept them without food for more than a day. We had just finished a substantial tea when a maid announced that two crofters wished to speak to the master of the house. He was a tall, muscular man, giving an impression of strength and determination as he strode out of the room. From a small back window that commanded a good view of the courtyard I had an opportunity of seeing what passed. The two men approached him in a menacing attitude. They seemed to know where their horses were imprisoned. A keen struggle, not unlike a Rugby scrum, ensued; but the attackers, being two to one, gained the victory. They burst open the locked door, only to find themselves made prisoners along with the horses. Then arose shouts and threats, mingled with forcible Gaelic imprecations. In time they realised that they had got the worst of the contest, for their language began to take a more subdued and apologetic tone. In the end they were permitted to retrieve their horses on promising to keep them off the farm lands in the future. When the farmer, heated and perspiring, rejoined us in the parlour, I was amused at what caused him a sense of regret—namely, that he could not bring himself to smash with his iron-toed boot the fingers of the man who unthinkingly grasped the bottom of the door in his endeavour to wrench it open. Men will do cruel things when the blood is up. Personally, I was glad I had not seen him perform this act of cruelty.

Let me conclude this chapter with an amusing episode connected with the marines. A number of them in charge of a sergeant were encamped beside the manse of Barvas, about fourteen miles from Stornoway. Most of them were well-knit, handsome fellows. The native lassies, though they naturally detested their presence in the island, could not help admiring them in their scarlet coats. Bright colours have always appealed to the Celtic nature. The scullery of the manse had a small window facing the courtyard, in which the sergeant was frequently to be seen. Though the glass had received a coat of white lead to tone down the light, the maidservant, like meddlesome Matty, being of an inquisitive nature, contrived to scrape off as much as enabled her to peep out to where the soldiers were encamped. Her surprise may be imagined when one night as she placed her eye to the peep-hole she detected another eye on the outside. It appeared that two could play at the peeping game. The sequel was a wedding, and I think I am correct in stating that more than one Lewis lass found a husband in a good-looking member of the red-coated marines.

But everything comes to an end. So did these stirring times. The crofters became reconciled to their lot when the island, along with others, was visited by the Crofter Commissioners, who adjusted rents and granted many concessions beneficial to the townships.

The year before I visited the island for the last time in the summer of 1888, the expenses incurred by the School Boards of the four parishes had become so burdensome that the members, unable to meet their obligations, threw up their task. Thus the education machine was on the verge of coming to a standstill. This could not be allowed. Accordingly, the Department adopted a system of special interventions, so as to give it direct control. Dr. John Lindsay Robertson, H.M. Inspector of Schools, also a native of Lewis, was appointed administrator. He was of necessity a manager of the school districts where educational difficulties existed. His position was unique. He had to examine the schools, appraise the grants, and see to their judicious disbursement. To improve matters, it became a case of raking in as much money as possible with one hand and paying out as little as possible with the other. All the same, he dealt well by the teachers. His administration was eminently successful, and fully justified an appointment in which his Gaelic-speaking colleagues heartily acquiesced.

Chapter XII

ORKNEY

I had heard much of the efficiency of the Orkney schools, so it was with pleasurable feelings that I was informed that I was to assist the Inspector in charge of the district in the summer of 1889. A glorious experience it certainly proved to be, when one was so far removed from the 'justlings of the world.' During the eight weeks I was there not a drop of rain fell.

In those days convenience demanded that the inspection of the schools should be effected by sailing from island to island in a sloop specially chartered for the purpose. It was named the *Elizabeth*, and belonged to one Captain Campbell, a native born and bred, who knew every island, and, what was of more importance, all the treacherous currents with which every Orcadian mariner is familiar. A more trustworthy man never put foot on a sailing vessel. His aim was to make the progress of the Inspector as easy and pleasant as possible. In this he succeeded admirably.

In the sloop on either side of the small cabin was a berth or 'bunk' in which we slept. The hold, having the floor well bedded with heather, was converted into a dressing-room and lavatory. In the forecastle were quartered the Captain and his crew of two hands, one of whom was old Dauvit, the cook.

The schools on the mainland were visited first. This

done, we took up our quarters on the *Elizabeth* and set sail from Kirkwall, visiting each island in turn. Incidentally, I may mention that our other 'hand' was a lad of sixteen, who, suffering from a bad cold, coughed so loudly and persistently of a night, as we lay at anchor, that we could get no sleep. To get rid of this nuisance the captain had to put him ashore for good. This he reluctantly did, as the lad was evidently a favourite, and had been looking forward to a cruise of the islands.

The weather was exceptionally warm and sunny. We did not require to concern ourselves much about stores. What we did lay in were sugar, tea, and such things as we might have found some difficulty in procuring in the islands visited. Fowls, milk, butter, and eggs, all of the best quality, could be obtained at any time, and that, too, at small cost.

A more hospitable people than the Orcadians could not be met with anywhere. We seldom required to take lunch on board, for the teachers' wives were always careful to have an appetising meal in readiness against the conclusion of the examination. Orkney is a land of fowls, so it was rare if a tender chicken was not an item of the menu. Indeed, a joke went round that the fowls all took to roost when the Inspector's sloop appeared in the offing. That the feast was sometimes spread on the previous evening we had proof, for one night we dropped into a schoolhouse on the island of Sanday on a business matter. There, laid temptingly on a table, was the morrow's lunch, including the never-failing cold 'chuckie.' Being hungry, I cast longing eyes on it; but patience had to be exercised, so I passed the night in pleasurable anticipation of at least one hearty meal next mid-day.

We were never without fresh fish, cod, haddock, ling, etc., all of our own catching. Let me here recount an incident of which I have pleasant memories. It was a broiling, hot morning when we were becalmed off the Red Head of Eday. At four o'clock I was sweltering in my berth, when I heard the Captain shouting down the stairway, "Are you coming up, Mr. Wilson? There's plenty of fish." Always a keen sportsman, especially where fishing was concerned, I immediately sprang up, and, clad in nothing save my night-shirt, I scrambled on deck. I feel that deck yet, under a blazing sun, hot as a baking griddle. I at once got to work. To the end of a long, thin rope like a gardener's line was attached a mass of lead shaped somewhat like the weight of a grandfather clock. A few scrapes with a knife caused the sides of it to glisten like silver. Tied to the weight with short stout cords were a number of big hooks. Slowly I lowered this contrivance of destruction over the gunwhale till it struck the bottom. Then drawing it up about a yard, I began a backward and forward motion of the line, thus causing the lead to dart up and down. The fish, always inquisitive when anything glitters, rush forward to investigate, with the result that a hook is almost certain to find its home somewhere about the head. In less time than it takes to tell the fish is writhing on the warm deck, to be seized by Dauvit, whose task is to gut and salt the catch near the bow. I may add that the instrument I have described is known as the 'murderer' or 'ripper,' a most appropriate name.

In those days the contrast between the conditions of the Hebrides and Orkney Islands was remarkable. In the former one was struck with the comparative poverty of the bulk of the people, whereas in the latter the prevailing tone was comfort and contentment. Here the natives, particularly on the mainland, frequently owned their own farms and crofts. It was customary to speak of the hundred lairds of the parish of Harray. In Dounby school the fathers of almost all the pupils owned their own land. Seeing the comfortable circumstances and prosperity of the people one might be pardoned for wondering why the Orkney Islands were classed with the Hebrides for certain extra school grants.

The Orcadians are not Celts. Their language proclaims them to be of Norse descent. To them Gaelic is a foreign tongue. Previous to my visit the Scottish Education Code made it plain that for a 'pass' in Reading the pupil had to read 'with expression.' Had this injunction of My Lords been carried out, not a child would have passed in North Ronaldsay, the most northerly of the group. This island was known of old as Rinansey. The name St. Ringan, after one of St. Columba's followers, clung to it, even after the wave of Norse paganism had spread over the Orkney Islands. The accent of the natives is so strongly Norse that a mainland Orcadian cannot help smiling when he hears a North Ronaldsay man speaking. It sounds abrupt and expressionless.

To reach the school on this remote island we had no end of trouble. Starting one morning from the head of Otterswick Bay with every stitch of canvas spread, for there was barely a breeze to fill the sail, we headed for South Bay in North Ronaldsay. About mid-day we were off Whitemill Point. Here our worries began. Lack of wind and strong-running, adverse currents compelled us to return to our starting place. As our intended visit had been duly intimated, we saw in the far distance a white bed sheet hoisted on a pole near the school. This was the signal that the pupils were assembled and waiting for us. Conditions were rather promising next morning, when we once more hoisted sail. By afternoon we were well into North Ronaldsay Firth. But, as bad luck would have it, the wind again fell, and we got into a current that carried us away to the north-west, with every prospect of finding ourselves ultimately in the Arctic Ocean. The Captain, thoroughly disgusted, exhausted every device in his nautical repertoire to stay our progress northward. I even saw old Dauvit sticking his knife in the mast to bring wind. Nor am I ashamed to say I also tried whistling, which I had been told was sometimes effective. But Aeolus would not be coaxed. About five o'clock in the afternoon the current changed, but the drift towards the island was so slow that, when about four miles off the coast, I suggested rowing ashore in our small boat or dinghy. It was really a case of take to the oars when there is no wind. The white sheet was meanwhile floating in what breeze there was, so we knew we should have no difficulty in getting the pupils. I may mention that on the previous evening we saw it flying up till nine o'clock. Now commenced a terrible pull, not with nice, light racing oars, but with long, heavy sweeps, such as are used on big barges and sloops. Dauvit was left alone on board with instructions to drift into South Bay if he could. As we rowed away, leaving the sloop with every stitch of canvas set and the solitary old man standing at the helm, a picture that

Coleridge would have gloated upon, I thought we had done a risky thing. However, we were determined to reach the island. This we managed to do about 7 p.m. Every pupil was present, and the examination passed off successfully. While in school the footgear of the pupils attracted my attention. It consisted of a sort of slippers made of raw hide. Those worn by one girl were particularly pretty, showing considerable skill and artistic taste. She told me her father made them, and on my admiring them the teacher undertook to supply me with a new pair before I left. This he did. They are called *rivelins*, and are possibly worn there to this day.

As one approaches North Ronaldsay, from which the Fair Isle, belonging to the Shetland group, can be seen, what strikes him most is the barrier wall of rough stones surrounding the island. This is erected to keep out the small breed of bedraggled-looking sheep that feed at the ebb tide on the brine-soaked seaweeds. The rich grass inland is not for them. It is the portion of the cows and horses.

Orkney abounds in curious place-names, mostly derived from the Norse. Names of places ending in 'bister' and 'quoy' are common. Not less striking are the names of persons. In one school on the mainland I came across the surnames Stove and Matches. As a rule the pupils were bright and more intelligent than one would have expected, seeing that they had never seen a train or tramcar. Very few outside the mainland had ever seen 'the tree' which grows in a street in Kirkwall. It is not generally known that trees do not grow in the Hebrides, Orkney and Shetland Islands, except a few stunted specimens in quiet nooks which have escaped the fierce blasts sweeping in from the surrounding ocean.

South-west of North Ronaldsay lies Sanday, an island interesting in many ways. It was here that I saw cow dung, that had lain in the fields till it was baked hard in the sun, used as fuel. I felt the flavour of it in the oatcakes. I was told that in days of old, when lighthouses in Orkney were not so numerous as they are now, the natives benefited much from shipwrecks. It is said that one pawky minister of Sanday prayed that there might be no shipwrecks; but he added, "Oh, Lord, if there are to be any, in Thy great mercy don't forget the poor people of Sanday."

I had proof when here that the children were of a kindly nature and well disposed towards their everyday friends the beasts and birds. I was crossing the playground of Lady School, when at one point the teacher, who was accompanying me, suddenly pulled me aside in case I should put my foot on a lark sitting on her nest amongst the dry, sunburnt grass. When I expressed astonishment at seeing a nest in the very heart of the playground, he assured me that the girls often played jingo-ring, dancing with joined hands, round and round the bird, which was in no way perturbed. The incident reminded me of my having seen a swallow's nest at a school in Stirlingshire above the lobby door by which the pupils entered and left. These incidents of consideration for birds were in sharp contrast to the case of the Glasgow boys who were spending their holidays in the island of Jura. Here in the inn a young pet seal had its home. As it was disporting itself in its natural element one day these rascals found pleasure in cruelly stoning it to death.

Swona is a very small island in the Pentland Firth. It is

so sparsely peopled that the children have to be taught by an itinerant teacher. When I was in Orkney they had to cross in a boat to be examined in the nearest public school in the island of South Ronaldsay. As it happened the day was fine and the passage pleasant for both the fair-haired, blue-eyed children and the fathers who accompanied them. During the examination the latter, anxious to see how it fared educationally with their offspring, seated themselves on a form by the wall at my back. One bright-looking youngster was being examined in Geography along with others belonging to the main school. His answers showed that he was far and away the cleverest boy in the group. His father, noting how his son moved step by step to the top of the class, became so excited that he could not restrain himself, so he blurted out, "Weel done, Johnny! Weel done, my laddie!" Instead of calling him to order, as would have been inevitable in a court of justice, I promptly endorsed his sentiments. That night, I feel convinced, would be a memorable one, when the incident was discussed, as it was sure to be, by the firesides of windswept Swona.

Off the north-west coast of Stronsay lies the small uninhabited island of Linga. Here seals, eider ducks and other aquatic birds are to be found in great abundance. The long grass which covers the island affords excellent nesting places for the eider ducks. It was on a Saturday afternoon that we dropped anchor in the sound which separates the two islands. Uninhabited islands had ever a fascination for me, so in the quiet, summer evening I made up my mind to land on Linga. Donning a pair of long-topped seaman's boots, and accompanied by the Captain and Dauvit, I rowed ashore. We each carried a pail in which to deposit the eggs which we were certain of finding at that season. I have been on many uninhabited islands on the coast of Scotland; but on this occasion, for a reason I am unable to explain, I could not shake off a depressing sense of loneliness. Perhaps this may have been accentuated by my visiting the ruins of what had once been a dwelling from which as I approached it there emerged with a whirring sound, similar to that emanating from an aeroplane, thousands of starlings. Eider ducks' nests were numerous. The female would sit on her clutch of about nine big, green-shelled eggs till one almost trod upon her before she took flight, leaving behind her a most repulsive aroma. The nests were composed of beautiful, soft breast feathers, which, when handled, reminded one of the old-fashioned Tam o' Shanter caps. Our pails being filled, we betook ourselves to the sloop. That night, before I slept, I requested Dauvit to place a selection of the eggs on the table for our Sunday breakfast. I have no doubt Dauvit had his own thoughts regarding the condition of the eggs as he placed a goodly, well-boiled basinful before us next morning. But he had barely cleared the stairway when something like a shower of eider ducks' eggs went streaming over his head into the sea. This of course resulted from my opening two or three to find them either full of feathers or addled. It was long after this before I could bring myself to contemplate a duck's egg, particularly if it happened to be of a greenish hue, with anything approaching complacency. Writing of Orkney and eider ducks, I am reminded of the great auk, or, as Dean Munro calls it, the 'gair fowl.' Martin, when in St. Kilda in 1697, thus describes it: "It is the stateliest as well as the largest sort—wings short, and flies not at all. Its egg is twice as big as that of the solan goose," etc. The only other place in Great Britain where it had its abode was the Orkneys. It is recorded that in 1812 Mr. Bullock hunted one without success off the small island of Papa Westray, lying northeast of Pierowall. I had read this, and made a point of visiting the ledge of rock on which tradition has it the female bird had her nest for the last time before she was killed. This, however, by the way.

In Westray itself I found much that was interesting. We arrived at the small pier at Pierowall, a fair-sized village. After the examination of the school I took a walk up the sloping road to view the ruins of Noltland Castle, which is historically one of the most interesting in Orkney. It is a huge pile with a large square tower containing a staircase of long stone steps, having loopholes so arranged that it would have been impossible for an enemy to ascend without being killed. It was built in the fifteenth century by Thomas de Tulloch, Bishop of Orkney, and in its day was the most northerly building of architectural interest in Britain. History records that at one time it belonged to Adam Bothwell, Bishop of Orkney, who conveyed it to Sir Gilbert Balfour of Westray, master of the household of Mary Queen of Scots. This Adam Bothwell was also Commandator of Holyrood. It was he who married the unfortunate Queen to his cousin, the well-known Bothwell, who figures so much in the latter part of her career in Scotland. It is also recorded that Nortland Castle was intended by Bothwell to be an asylum for Queen Mary. Be that as it may, there it stands laden with history. Could it speak it could tell many a thrilling tale. The farmer, whose house stands across the road facing the ruin, drew my attention to a spot far up on the face of the tower, where there was an oblong of stones much smaller in size than those used in the construction of the building. He told me there was a local tradition that, in reward for the excellence of his plan, the owner slew the architect and deposited his body behind this obvious oblong of small stones. By this cruel act he was determined to make certain that none of the secrets of the construction of the castle would ever be divulged. Whether the tale be true or not, in that far-off island it would be very difficult to make the tower reveal its secret. It is sometimes more interesting to accept tradition than to destroy it. The castle was burned in 1745, and it has remained a ruin ever since.

Since I was in Orkney, Birsay, on the north-west of the mainland, has become famous. Seated on Marwick Head, four hundred feet above the western ocean, I recalled the lines in Coleridge's monody on the death of Chatterton:

Anon, upon some rough rock's fearful brow
Would pause abrupt, and gaze upon the waves below.

The tide had ebbed to its limit, disclosing reef after reef of ugly rocks stretching far out into the Atlantic. Here Lord Kitchener met his doom, when the *Hampshire* went down in 1916. When I heard of the tragedy I felt convinced that on a coast like this, with a terrific north-wester blowing, such as was the case on that fateful night, no vessel could possibly be in a more dangerous locality.

Before concluding this chapter, let me say something of Hoy, the hilly island of Orkney. There are two schools here. The smaller one is situated on the western seaboard in the neighbourhood of the Old Man of Hoy, a famous, high, isolated rock commemorated in song by the late Professor Blackie:

> *The Old Man of Hoy*
> *Looks out on the sea,*
> *Where the tide runs strong and the wave rides free:*
> *He looks on the broad Atlantic sea.*

After I had inspected the larger school on the north side, I bent my steps to the valley on the eastern slope of which, opposite the Wardlaw Hill, the highest in the island, lies the Dwarfie Stone referred to in *The Pirate* by Sir Walter Scott. As I mounted through the heather, I became obsessed with the intense solitude of my surroundings. I recalled John Malcolm the poet's description of it:

> *There bosomed in a deep recess*
> *Sleeps a dim vale of loneliness;*
> *The circling hills all bleak and wild*
> *Are o'er its slumbers darkly piled.*

At last I came upon the object of my search. Nor was this difficult, for there was no stone approaching it in size on the hillside. In appearance it was a large, flattish boulder, said to be thirty feet long, about fifteen wide, and from five to six feet in height. Lying in front of it was a large cube-shaped stone opposite an aperture. Entering, I found a bed-like excavation on either side of a short passage. How the stone came to be where it is nobody can tell. Its history is wrapped in complete obscurity, yet its existence has for centuries been well known. Countless visitors have seen it; amongst them Hugh Miller, who carved his name inside one of the recesses. There is a tradition that long ago a dwarf took up his abode inside it; hence its name.

Chapter XIII
THE LIGHTER
SIDE

I t was often the lot of the Inspector to have his
progress enlivened by some humorous anecdote or
episode. It was on a cold, blustering morning in
December that I boarded the steamer at
Campbeltown on my way to Gourock. I exchanged
opinions with the Captain on the character of the weather.
He predicted a rough passage once we got past Davaar
Island at the entrance to the bay. Betaking myself to the
cabin, I found I was then the sole passenger. I had thus an
opportunity of selecting the most comfortable corner seat.
Collecting all the cushions I could lay hands on, I wrapped
myself in my plaid and lay down, prepared to face the
worst. Before we left the quay, however, to my surprise a
young woman with a baby in her arms made her appearance. Like myself, she too sought comfort, and noting that I
had secured the cosiest corner of the cabin, she approached
me with the request that, as she was sure to be seasick on
such a morning, I would oblige her by taking charge of her
baby. I at once foresaw very awkward possibilities. But,
while I could not bring myself to undertake such a respon-
sibility, I was quite willing to assist her in an endeavour to
meet a possible contingency. Springing up, I made useful

suggestions while she bolstered up her offspring amongst the cushions in the corner I had vacated. Here she left it and seated herself by the small stove which served to heat up the cabin. As I strolled round I pondered that as there was no stewardess on board there was some likelihood after all of my having to minister to the wants of that infant, and possibly of the mother herself. I was in anything but a peaceful frame of mind, when relief came. Another female made her appearance. Fleeing from the cabin, I betook myself to the deck, thus escaping, as events turned out, what would have been one of the most humiliating and ludicrous incidents of my career—namely, a bachelor School Inspector wrestling with a fractious, screaming baby in the cabin of a coasting steamer.

One tourist season the Inspector of the district was visiting Arisaig officially. All the hotel conveyances were in commission, so he had to visit his school on foot. To shorten the journey, he was informed that at a certain point he could be ferried across Loch nan Uamh in a crofter's boat. He found the crofter, and explained his desire to be taken to the other side. The latter, eyeing him all over before deciding, beckoned to a fellow-crofter who was loafing in the 'offing.' He evidently required this man to assist him to row the boat. Between the two a *sotto voce* discussion in Gaelic followed. They were evidently puzzled as to who the stranger might be. Finally, they concluded that he must be one of the tourist fraternity with plenty of money at his disposal. The Inspector, himself a Gaelic-speaking Celt, however, was following every word. He had asked them the cost of the ferry, though he knew all the time it was five shillings. As he waited for an answer he leisurely smoked his pipe, for he was a man who 'hurried no man's cattle.' He overheard the following dialogue in Gaelic: "He is asking the price." "Well, Angus, ask a pound." "What do you think he is?" "He looks like a Sassenach tourist." "Ach, but a pound will be too much." "No, he is a gentlemans." "Come along," said the Inspector, now becoming impatient; "how much is it to be?" "A pound," came the half-hearted reply. "All right," said the Inspector. The boat was launched, and the two rascals proceeded to row vigorously, the while interspersing personal observations about their passenger with remarks in Gaelic about the gullibility of strangers in the tourist season. Their tune, however, came to an abrupt conclusion. When about half-way across the loch a large bird rose from the water and winged its way across their heads. Seeing it, the Inspector, sitting smoking his pipe in the stern, asked in a loud voice in Gaelic, *"Ciod e an ian tha 'n sin?"* (What bird is that?) *"Scarabh!"* (cormorant) answered the nearest man, and down went the two heads, which they never raised till they reached the shore. Nor did either of them utter another word in Gaelic or English. They realised that they had been found out, and were evidently ashamed. With some forcible language in Gaelic bearing on the dishonesty of his countrymen the Inspector paid them five shillings, which they accepted without demur or any expression of gratitude.

It was on the occasion of my first visit to Durness, near Cape Wrath, in Sutherlandshire, that the Inspector of the district, whom I was assisting, met with a disappointment. Travelling from Tongue in a wagonette and pair, we lunched at Erriboll Farm, where we baited the horses. We then set out to complete the long journey. Near the head of Loch Erriboll, at the Inspector's suggestion, we halted and proceeded to place in the conveyance a quantity of fair-sized stones. The driver, without instructions, also got down and followed our example. To me this preparation betokened something exciting in store. I was told that from the crofters' houses scattered along the west side of the loch mongrel dogs of all colours, shapes and sizes were likely to rush out and by their ferocious barking tend to frighten the horses. The Inspector, who had frequently experienced exhibitions of their dangerous nature, deemed it expedient to be forearmed. With the stones it was intended at all hazards to subdue their notorious ferocity. I was promised what would help to relieve the monotony of a tedious journey, so I waited in suspense. The result, however, proved rather disappointing, for comparatively few dogs appeared for the predicted attack as we passed cottage after cottage. Those that did make a show got their due deserts, and 'the subsequent proceedings interested them no more.' But I must not omit to mention one white and black mongrel of the collie breed that did not fail to show himself. He was reputed to be a ringleader. Emerging at a safe distance, he cleverly evaded the anticipated missiles, and rushing across the road in front of the horses, made a snap at their noses. Then disappearing over a ridge, he crossed the road again a few yards farther on, repeating the same mordacious attitude. This mode of intermittent attack he practised for at least a mile. When we reached the hotel at Durness the lack of enthusiasm which we had just witnessed in the Loch Erriboll canine fraternity was explained. The Inspector of Salmon Fisheries had traversed the same road before us, and had passed Erriboll Farm while we were at lunch. He and his driver had laid on the stones so effectively that the ardour of the brutes was temporarily subdued. Only the most daring had enthusiasm enough left to assume the offensive a second time.

Here I may mention that in remote districts where strangers are few the risk of being bitten by dogs was always to be reckoned with. I have been bitten several times; but the worst wound I ever got was in one of the Hebridean Islands. The collie seized my arm, inflicting a nasty cut. Luckily in my company was a doctor, who had seen many cases of hydrophobia in India. He at once examined the wound, and assured me that no evil effects would follow, for the dog's teeth had been cleaned as they penetrated the cloth before reaching the skin. Luckily nothing serious supervened.

Only those who have been brought up on a sheep farm know how prone these animals are to imitate a leader. I have seen a ewe jump over a wooden box, and when it was removed every sheep following leap in precisely the same way over an imaginary obstacle at the identical spot. But I never laughed more heartily, and perhaps I shouldn't, than I did one evening at Dunvegan pier in Skye when I was returning from Canna. Half a dozen crofters with as many dogs had brought about thirty sheep along the pier to be shipped for Oban. By bad luck, one leading ewe happened to jump into the sea just behind the stern. Immediately one after another of the whole flock followed suit. It reminded me of people rushing to the rescue of a drowning man. The shouting, the barking of dogs and the waving of sticks were of no avail to stop the stampede. In fact they only increased it. No power on earth could have kept them back. However, they floated well, and by smart boat work they were driven to land and ultimately shipped to their destination.

Uig Lodge, on the far west side of Lewis, where the Inspector of the district and I used to sojourn for a week at a time when the shootings were unlet, was in charge of a tall, reliable native female, with whom I associate a huge basket of peats by the fireside and tempting, newly-baked scones. She was always pleased to see us, and did her best to make us comfortable. In a cottage within the grounds lived Kenny, the gamekeeper, who passed his leisure hours practising on a tub-toned violin. Of an evening, while we were there, he was invited across to the lodge to entertain us with some music, for which we were very grateful in that remote corner of Lewis. Living so far from civilisation, Kenny, who probably seldom had an opportunity of imbibing spirituous liquor, since the shootings were unlet, could not bring himself to refuse as many drams as were offered him, and he could stand a goodly number without 'turning a hair,' as they say. However, one night he over-stepped discretion be absorbing more than he could conveniently carry. When at last the bow flew from his grasp he had just utterance enough to apologise. Struggling to his feet and maintaining a measure of perpendicularity, he made for the door. In case of accident I took the precaution to see him safely inside his own cottage door. Here follows the humorous aspect of the tale. At that season it was never really dark in these latitudes. Next morning as I was taking a stroll before breakfast, whom should I meet but Kenny, looking rosy and exceedingly alert. When I naturally enquired how he had slept, he surprised me by replying, "Ach, I did not go to bed at all. I just took my gun and went away to shoot a peregrine falcon on Suainabhal that would be killing the grouse." Now this mountain is 1250 feet in height. To reach it he had to traverse trackless moors and bogs. After that he had to climb the mountain, whose steep rocky face rendered stalking a bird of prey exceedingly difficult and dangerous. "And did you get the peregrine?" I asked. "Ach, and to be sure I did. He will be killing no more grouse whatever." So this was the gamekeeper's method of working off the effects of a debauch to which in his isolation he was quite unaccustomed. I have frequently noted that solitude begets hardihood and a wonderful spirit of independence.

I was once talking to a gentleman who had just returned from a funeral at Taynuilt. I have been told that the soil in parts of the burying-ground is rather shallow. On this occasion the grave happened to be unusually deep. To those who for reasons of their own considered that a shallow grave would be ultimately advantageous this was disquieting. One farmer was heard to remark to his neighbour as they left the churchyard, "It's not fair, Colin, to bury Donald so deep an' him fou' o' rheumatics. We'll a' be throu' the Pass o' Brander afore he gets to the top." He evidently anticipated an eastward trek at the Resurrection.

It was at the end of the session that the children were being addressed by an enlightened member of a School

Board who had a wooden leg. To impress the boys with what can be accomplished by intelligent application and perseverance, he referred to his artificial limb in these words: "You all see that leg. Well, would you believe it, I made it oot o' my ain heid." To his bewilderment the laughter was loud and long. He concluded that he was being taken for either a boaster or a liar, till a clergyman at his elbow made a whispered explanation. He then saw the joke, and joined heartily in the prevailing hilarity.

Most people, in Scotland at least, are aware that Cromarty is the birthplace of Hugh Miller. Here a monument to his memory is erected on a rising ground. I was walking along the principal street one afternoon. A little in front of me was Hugh's son, also an eminent geologist. As two fishermen's boys passed me I heard one of them remark to his companion, "Ye see thon man, Tam?" "Aye!" "Weel, he's a *son* o' the moniment."

I heard a good story of a teacher whose school I used to examine. When on holiday he always 'did himself well.' On one occasion he was travelling on a west coast steamer and freely patronising the "canteen.' While doing so he fraternised with two commercial travellers, who secretly confided to another bagman that this loquacious individual was a dominie on the loose. The commercials then, for their diversion, concocted a little plot. The third man was to approach the teacher, and, representing himself as one of Her Majesty's Inspectors, was to upbraid him for his disreputable condition, and at the same time threaten to report him to My Lords of the Education Department. This he did much to the dismay and trepidation of the dominie. Later, however, one of them let the latter into the secret of the plot. Instantly Mac's dander was up, for he hated to be befooled. Without uttering a word he hurried on deck in search of Her Majesty's Inspector, whom he found leisurely surveying the seagulls that were following the steamer as he chuckled to himself on the effect of his little joke. But he got an unexpected surprise when Mac felled him with a terrific blow on the nose as he shouted, "You can put that into your next report to My Lords."

The children of gamekeepers and shepherds far removed from public schools had to be taught by itinerant, non-certificated teachers in their own homes. I used to derive much pleasure from my visits to these. The room end of the house was generally arranged for the ordeal, after which the Inspector was hospitably entertained by the parents. These were called side schools. The small school in Glen Etive, about three miles from the head of Loch Etive, fell into this category. To reach it the postman's motor boat had to be hired from Taynuilt. Here the scenery is about as grand and picturesque as any in the Highlands. So like is it to the Norwegian fjords that one year a large cinema company journeyed there to carry through that part of Marie Corelli's novel *Thelma* where the scene is laid in Norway. The postman's motor boat took them to and from the scene of their operations. I made a point of witnessing the film in Glasgow, and could not refrain from laughing at the fakes so cleverly effected in places with which I was so very familiar. There was the postman's old useless boat floating away with an old sail hoisted, and some of his old clothes stuffed with straw to represent the dead Viking lying on the deck. The whole was on fire, having been well saturated with paraffin before the sail was set. Not the least laughable part was the wretched dwarf committing suicide by leaping into the waterfall represented by a pair of the postman's stuffed trousers and vest tumbling down the Falls of Cruachan. To me it was all too comical for words; but the illusion was perfect and certainly thrilling. Being so much in the know, I thoroughly enjoyed it.

It is remarkable how little some children have seen outside their own environment. But if they are ignorant of the innumerable things that create intelligence in town children, they have compensation in their knowledge of the natural phenomena as well as the fauna and flora character-istic of their own neighbourhood. I remember examining a side school girl who lived in a wild glen so inaccessible that she had hardly ever spoken to a man other than her own father. I was questioning her orally in arithmetic by herself in order to let her home as soon as possible, for I saw that a storm was brewing on the arm of the sea that had to be crossed in an open boat. She stared hard at me and answered in an abrupt, challenging tone of voice. Being convinced that she would be familiar with hens, I asked her the price of six dozen eggs at fourpence halfpenny a dozen. "But they're too cheap," she at once replied. Not contradicting her, I waited for the answer, which after a pause came out correctly, to be followed by other questions of a more difficult character. Before I had finished with her I could not help concluding that she took me for a fool, and would doubtless be interest-ed to know what breed of fowls I kept that laid eggs so freely that I could sell them at such a cheap rate.

I was once driving in a wagonette and pair on the west side of Sutherlandshire, when I overtook a group of nine side school pupils in charge of their teacher walking along the hillside to the school I was going to inspect. Hearing the sound of the horses' hoofs, they naturally all turned round. My surprise was great when I saw a little chap about eight years of age dart from his companions. Rushing up the hill amongst the heather, he shouted in Gaelic *"Tha feagal orm"* (The fear is on me). Arrived at the school, I had it explained to me that till that day he had never seen a horse. He was a shepherd's son, living far away in the heart of the mountains. I overtook the same group on my return journey. Stopping the conveyance, I had the youngster hoisted to the box beside the driver. I see him yet with his small Glengarry bonnet as he sat clutching the cushion, and never for one moment taking his eyes off the prancing steeds till he was deposited at a wayside cottage to await the arrival of his companions. That night by the fireside his account in Gaelic of the examination would be eclipsed by his description of the two huge beasts which had occasioned him so much trepidation.

The migration of parents sometimes results in the number of children attending the school being greatly reduced. One school on Loch Lomond side occurs to me. Here the number fell off till one boy was left, who gradually discovered that he was in the unique position of being able to dictate to his teacher. He even went the length of fixing the holidays. I was told that of an afternoon he would sidle up to her and naïvely inform her that she could have a holiday. On her asking for an explanation of this unexpected information he would reply, "Because I'm nae comin' to the school the morn." But his career of independence did not last long. In due course other pupils came on the scene, and the teacher once more got the whip-hand of him.

In the days when the date of the inspection of the school had to be intimated beforehand it was common for the Inspector to find the schoolroom floor soaking wet with an overpowering aroma of carbolic acid. This condition of the atmosphere was not conducive to good temper. But window cleaning, a very important matter, was generally neglected. This reminds me of a somewhat unusual request made by a female teacher of middle age in a very picturesque western island. Finding the lonely situation of her school rather depressing, she asked permission from the school managers to marry a man. The latter, overflowing with compassion, but devoid of generosity sufficient to augment her salary as an inducement to retain her services, readily agreed provided a man's presence on the premises was not prejudicial to the interests of the school. Taking every risk, she married a man. I happened to visit the school shortly after the wedding, and as I crossed the playground I observed a very muscular specimen of the male sex perched on a ladder beside a window. Such a sight was unusual. Being interested after what I had heard of the teacher's matrimonial intentions, I asked one of the senior girls who he was. With a chuckle she replied, "Oh, that's the mistress' man, cleaning the windows with his big black beard." It was evident that his industrious wife was turning her bargain to good account. If there be any truth in the old tag that 'a hairy man's a happy man,' he to outward appearance justified his being placed in that category.

Let me conclude with two mirth provoking anecdotes with the inspectorate. At the end of each week an Inspector has to submit a diary giving the mileage travelled and the expenses incurred. Amongst these are charges for 'cabs' and 'porterage,' but these words are to be written after the amount charged. One doughty Inspector, thinking it sufficient, wrote simply 'porter.' Back came the diary with a statement that My Lords did not allow anything for refreshment. The Inspector was naturally irritated, knowing as he did that My Lords understood the legitimate nature of the charge. At the same time he knew that there was nothing to be gained by kicking against the pricks, so he affixed the missing *age* to porter, and added, "I daresay after this I shall have to write 'cabage' instead of 'cab.'"

Another time a diary official in London made the discovery from a map that the school which this same Inspector had to travel three miles from his headquarters to reach was, as he put it, *one mile as the crow flies*. An explanation was required, and he got it. The Inspector, weighing about sixteen stones, wrote on the margin of the diary as follows: "The school is certainly a mile distant as the crow flies, but I am not a crow. Secondly, a wide and deep river flows between my residence and the school. I can swim, but my assistant can't. I could carry him on my back, but I am afraid he would not trust me; hence the charge for a conveyance."

Chapter XIV

THE UNEXPECTED

The days when the Inspector saw the pupils decked out in Sunday 'braws' are long past. Even in the Lewis schools, where the clothes worn at the visit were those of everyday wear, the girls often had their hair tied with a gaudy piece of ribbon purchased in Stornoway for the occasion. Here the attempts to improve matters were sometimes ludicrous in the extreme, as when the boys turned out in articles of clothing belonging to their fathers or elder brothers. A cap or jacket many sizes too large was ludicrous enough; but when it came to wearing their elders' wide trousers with the legs rolled up to the requisite length it was impossible to suppress a smile. One day a small boy in an infant class remained seated while his class-mates jumped up at the request of the teacher. Being desirous of knowing the nature of the ailment which necessitated this attitude, I asked the teacher for an explanation. She proceeded to investigate, and found that the youngster had on a pair of trousers belonging to an elder brother. Whilst seated he had contrived by drawing up his bare foot, probably for warmth, to get it into the seat of the trousers in such a way that rising was impossible. He was thus practically anchored to the seat.

The angle at which children view things is often

amusing when they are asked to set out their ideas in writing. For instance, a boy, describing the church he attended, wrote, "The gas is all at one end of the church. There is no light at the other end." Gaelic-speaking pupils, and those whose acquaintance with English is scant, sometimes express themselves in sentences full of unconscious humour. A Barra boy, describing the herring fishery, a local industry, adopted the language of Scripture, with which he was most familiar. He wrote, "And it came to pass that the fishermen rose early in the morning. They betook themselves to the west to get the big fish. And lo! the sun shone for behold he cometh. And the fish-curers said to one go and he goeth and to another come and he cometh. The lads and the gutters were waiting for them," etc. The use of lads reminds me that when I first visited Barra with the district Inspector, who was my senior by only two years, a pupil describing the examination wrote, "We had our own Inspector, and he had a *lad* with him." I felt sure I had begun to renew my youth.

Into what category could one place the pupil who wrote, "Wood is made of stick which grows on trees"; or one who thus described a corn, "The man had a corn as big as his wife's foot, it was so small"?

Defective hearing as well as lack of concentration often accounts for laughable blunders. A boy rendered the narrative of Christ and the tribute money in these words. "The men brought Him a coin. They thought He would know all about it. Christ just looked at it for a little and then said, 'Whose miserable subscription is this?'" This youth would doubtless have proved a valuable asset to the

Salvation Army. Another profanely rendered the text, "Casting all your cares upon Him for He careth for you," as "Catching all your carriage pownies for here's a carriage for you"; likewise, "He sitteth in the scorner's chair" as "He sitteth in his *corner* chair," probably due to his seldom having seen his grandfather out of it.

A twelve year old pupil of weakish intellect, who had got fairly jumbled in his knowledge of the Scriptures, wrote the following clotted stuff: "Jessie Bell (Jezebel) was a wicked woman. They did not like her at all. The King came in and told them to toss her out. They did it seventy times seven. And they took up the fragments that remained twelve baskets full. She did not do any ill after that." I should think not.

Perhaps no error is more frequent in the written composition of pupils than the misplacing of words and phrases. The result is often laughable, as when a youngster wrote, "He took a horse to the man with a saddle on his back," and again, "He sold the piano to an old lady with mahogany legs." The boy evidently did not grasp the predicament of the young farmer when he wrote, "The cow was the property of a young farmer due to calve in three months."

A girl with a curious mental twist, describing a motor accident, had this sentence, "The omnibus was always full of men; but this time the only man was a woman." Again a boy in Acharacle school in Argyll wrote, "There has not been a summer here for three years"; truly a deplorable state of matters in such a remote locality.

The oral answers are as a rule quite as ludicrous as the written. A pupil who viewed things from the negative side, when asked, "What is a cow?" answered, "Please, Mam, it's not a rabbit, nor a horse." His deduction was evidently from observation of the ears. A boy in a colliery district of Stirlingshire, when asked, "What is the difference between a man and a woman?" replied, "A man can stan' on's heid but a woman canna." Sifting out the reason for this answer, the teacher found that he had been recently at a variety entertainment, where he had made a special study of the acrobats.

One day a teacher wrote on the blackboard, 'James ate the jam,' and after explaining that James is a proper noun and jam a common one, to ascertain if the pupils grasped the distinction, she asked. "Now what is the difference?" From a bright youngster came the reply, "Please, Miss, you can eat the jam, but you can't eat James." The instruction was evidently missing its mark.

I heard a teacher explaining with great earnestness how the rind of an apple helped to keep in the juice. She concluded the lesson with, "Now, children, if I took off the rind and laid the apple on the window-sill for two days, what would happen?" An urchin conscious of the frailty of human nature, particularly in its incipient phase, replied in a subdued voice, "Please, Mam, it wudna be there."

The old Scottish proverb, 'Wee stoups hae lang lugs,' implies caution when conversing in the hearing of young-sters. A precocious boy whose father was a manual labourer had been listening to the talk by the fireside. When he was asked the meaning of the word 'sack,' which occurred in his reading lesson, he unhesitatingly replied, "If a man doesna do his wark he gets the sack."

Some unexpected answers are more amusing than others. I had the following from the female teacher of a class in a slum school. Whilst engaged in teaching an object lesson, she heard a knock at the door. Before opening it, bethinking herself of the possibility of a surprise visit from the Inspector, she cautioned the class against talking or making a noise in her absence. Speaking, however, did occur, and enquiry elicited the prompt information that Jeanie Smith was the culprit. "And what would you call Jeanie for disobeying me?" she asked. A small boy, using the unauthorised vocabulary of the home, at once replied, "A b—h"—the grammatical equivalent of a female dog—a word eschewed in polite society.

When a little girl was asked how she knew that she had been christened, she answered, "Because I hae the marks on my airm."

When requested to form sentences orally from a given theme, the pupils' answers often betray mental alertness full of unconscious humour. A class had been reading the account of a bear that some boys had seen robbing a bees' hive. At the conclusion the teacher invited them to form sentences embracing the words *boys*, *bees* and *bear*. A thoughtful youngster who had recently spent a holiday at the seaside unhesitatingly gave as his contribution, "Boys bes bare when they're bathing."

A teacher asked her infants to say something about a hen. One offered, "A hen lays eggs because she can't help it"; another, "Hens won't lay because it's too cold." But an amusing statement I often got when using a Cat for a theme was, "A cat lays kittens."

The answer that admits of no contradiction is sometimes due to the nature of the question. Thus, when a teacher asked why a certain great man was buried in Westminster Abbey, a bright Irish boy replied, "Because he was deid." One Inspector, asking how it came about that Queen Mary was born in Linlithgow, received as answer, "Because her mother was there at the time." In reply to the question, "Why did Mary and Darnley not agree?" he got, "Because he steyed oot at nicht in the Kirk field an' wudna come hame till's bed."

At the daily Bible lesson the teacher had been impressing on her girls the sin of swearing. During the play-hour one of them heard a boy using bad language. Knowing that this merited chastisement, she hurried to the class-room, and, approaching the teacher, she said in a state of excitement, "I say, Mam, Tommy Whyte said a bad word." "What did he say?" asked the teacher. After a thoughtful pause the precocious informant replied, "Oh! Mam, I can't say it, but if you say all the bad words you know I'll tell you when you come to it." What the child considered a sin in one of her own age did not appear to be heinous when uttered by the teacher, who could not even 'swear with a good grace.'

The written notes and excuses of parents sometimes afford much amusement, particularly in the case of those who seldom put pen to paper. I once found lying on a teacher's desk a mother's note which ran, "Please, Miss Hay, excuse Maggie being absent to-day as she died last Friday." The note was dated Monday. It is difficult to imagine what induced a parent to send such an unnecessary note. Another I once read was in these terms, written without a pause, 'Ples Miss —, excus Willie for being away he was helpin' me to wash Mrs. McRae." Writing of excuses for absence brings to my mind the story of a boy who, on being pressed for the reason why he was not present on the previous day, replied that his father was ill. "And what was the matter with him?" asked the teacher. This seemed to trouble him, but the teacher was insistent. In a little came, in a subdued voice, "The whuskey."

The teacher who received this note giving an excuse for absence might be excused for smiling when she read it: "Please don't whip Tommy for being absent yesterday. The baby burnt her handy and Tommy *flew* for the doctor and got a *soar* foot."

It looked as if the mother who had a boy at a so-called defective school was disappointed when informed of the result of the Inspector's test, for when a neighbour asked her how her boy had got on she replied in a despairing tone of voice, "Johnny has been examined for an idiot and failed."

Ignorance on the part of the parent is sometimes very irritating to the teacher. One who was instructing the girls in Domestic Economy received from the mother of one of them this note, "Miss—, be good enough not to tell Annie anything more about her intervals. It makes her nervish. Her stomach is bad enough already; she spued twice last night."

Nor does the medical officer escape the parents' wrath. One of them in a certain county deemed it necessary, through the teacher, to inform a parent that her boy suffered from mouth breathing. The reward for imparting this valuable piece of gratis information was a letter from the indignant mother couched in these terms, "Mistress, David is just as God made him: if you will change him in any way you will suffer for it at the great day of judgement."

The subject of good manners is frequently discussed in school, and not oftener than it ought to be. It is said that an aunt was visiting a school girl's parents, and, being interested in her education, she asked her if she was now learning anything new. "Ow, aye," said the wee lass, "we are learnin' menners noo. We are learnin' to *rift* ahint oor haun." I may be excused for explaining that *rift* in Scots for an emission of stomachic gas from the mouth, a process recognised as vulgar, particularly so if audibly emitted.

School jokes connected with the Inspector are legion. Here are a few. The Inspector should not be too hasty in drawing conclusions. When testing a class on their knowledge of Vulgar Fractions the Inspector asked a boy whether he would have half an orange or a quarter of one. To the teacher's dismay he preferred a quarter. From this the Inspector, who knew a boy's tastes in the matter of fruit, concluded that the instruction was not quite fundamentally thorough. But he was soon disillusioned. As he crossed the playground shortly afterwards he beckoned the youngster to him. Of course his class-mates crowded round, interested in the interview. The Inspector said, "Oh, you're the boy who would take a quarter of an orange rather than a half." He had hardly said this when a forward youngster at his elbow exclaimed, "Please, Sir, that laddie disna like oranges." This never occurred to Her Majesty's Inspector. No doubt the poor teacher got justice after all.

The Inspector was examining the pupils of a class individually. A boy came forward and placed his books on the table in front of him. They appeared to be very dirty. To impress the boy with this fact the Inspector, with his eyes fixed on them, commenced to roll up his sleeves, at the same time asking, "Why am I doing this?" The unexpected reply was, "Please, Sir, not to file (dirty) my books."

An Inspector who had laid special stress on good manners in children on one occasion found the tables turned on him. He had been examining a class, and had just left the room, when he discovered that he had left his notebook behind. He re-entered, and, crossing the floor space with a view to testing the observant faculties of the class, he asked, "Did any of you children notice what I forgot?" An eagle-eyed youngster at once said, "Yes, Sir, you forgot to say, 'Excuse me,' when you passed in front of Miss Smith." Though the Inspector blushed, I have no doubt the report on Miss Smith's class did not suffer on account of this unlooked-for reproof.

To encourage pupils to make personal remarks is always dangerous, but happily they seldom cause offence. An Inspector, delighted with the intelligence displayed by a class of infants, finished up with the heartening appeal, "Now, children, say anything you like about me." A young hopeful, probably struck with his clean appearance compared with that of his collarless father, at once offered, "You wear a dickie." And it was true.

The child's outspoken answer often betrays a certain amount of guilelessness, even when the question comes from a source likely to inspire awe and respect. Here is an instance. A genial Inspector entering a school met a little girl crying bitterly, with a companion consoling by her side. "And what is the matter with this poor girl?" asked the scholarly gentleman in a sympathetic tone of voice. The companion after a little hesitation answered pathetically, "Please, Sir, she has a sair guts." The language of the home came to the top. Forcefulness was certainly not sacrificed on the alter of politeness.

Sheep-shearing had just been concluded for the season, and a shepherd accompanied by his little daughter was paying a first visit to the Scottish Zoo. Arrived at the lion's cage, the girl, as soon as she saw the beautiful animal with his smooth, sleek skin and shaggy mane , exclaimed, "Oh, father, they've been clippin' the lion." Familiar as she was with sheep-shearing, the remark was only natural, but the task would have taken some doing.

I shall conclude this chapter with the story of a youngster who was evidently a budding philosopher. He was gathering stones in the garden beside his grandfather, who was busy digging. Something prompted him to ask who made all the stones. To the old man's reply that God made all the stones came the next question, "Could he make a stone so big that He could not lift it?" This provided the old man with food for reflection. Either 'yes' or 'no' would not accord with the omnipotence of the Almighty, so without giving a definite answer he suggested that they should leave off work for the day.

Chapter XV
HOTELS

Greater facilities for travelling have resulted in the School Inspectors being less familiar sojourners at hotels than they used to be. On the whole a friendly feeling existed between them and commercial travellers, whom Sterne dubbed 'Peregrine Martyrs.' It was often cemented in the billiard or smoking-room.

In a northern hotel an Inspector of my acquaintance and a garrulous bagman, over a social glass, spent a very pleasant evening. Towards bedtime the latter, becoming elated through his companion's pleasantries, ventured to ask him the nature of his business. "I travel for stationery," said the Inspector. Next morning the Inspector's letters, with the legend 'On Her Majesty's Service' on the envelopes, were arranged on the mantelpiece against his arrival for breakfast. His convivial friend, who preceded him, noted the character of his correspondence. Accordingly, on the Inspector's entry, he quietly remarked, "Aye, aye, man, I wish I traivellt for as guid a house as yours."

In my experience, one of the greatest nuisances in hotels is the man who behaves as if the house belongs to him, and that every other person is there on sufferance. This individual finds delight in whistling and singing wherever

he goes. He seems to be obsessed with a desire to fill sonif-
erous corridors and staircases with sound, never turning a
thought to others to whom his ebullitions may be objectionable. I have even heard him shouting and whistling in his
bath, much to the annoyance of the occupant of the
adjoining bedroom. Mention of a bath brings to my recollection an amusing incident. A visitor to a Highland inn
where there was no bathroom ordered a bath to be brought
to his bedroom door next morning. This the maid-servant,
to whom a bath was anything but a luxury, was mindful to
do. She had hardly had time to go downstairs, however,
when there was a furious ringing of his bell. She hurried
upstairs in a state of consternation. On coming down she
met her mistress, who, certain that something serious had
happened, asked her what he wanted. "Water," replied the
innocent Hebe.

I was once in a Kinross hotel much frequented by men
fishing on Loch Leven. The house, when I arrived, was so
crowded that I had to take up my sleeping quarters in one
of two adjoining wood-lined garrets on the top storey. It
happened that I went to bed sooner than usual, as I had to
be up early to catch a train for Stirling. It turned out that
the adjoining room was the sleeping-place of two young
men hailing from over the Border. I had made myself as
comfortable as possible, and in the stillness prevailing at
that elevation had been asleep for about two hours, when I
was suddenly awakened by the noise of heavy feet
ascending the stairs. This was rendered all the more disagreeable by whistling and loud talking. But it was after the
disturbers had entered their room and slammed the door

that their behaviour became unbearable. At first they seemed to be wrestling with one another. Then they laughed and whistled while they were undressing. In a little the creaking of a bedstead indicated that they had surely come to rest at last. But this was not the case, for they kept up an animated discussion of the latest cricket results till nearly 3 a.m., when all was still. By this time my temper was strained to its utmost limit. I now lay and plotted revenge. To catch my train it was necessary for me to be up at 5 a.m. At this unearthly hour I rose and forthwith commenced to make things lively for my neighbours, who from their loud snoring I concluded were very sound asleep. While I was dressing I banged chairs in all directions, opened and slammed the door a few times, whistled, and sang every song, good, bad, or indifferent, I could think of, thus doing my best to make the state of matters beyond endurance. Suddenly the snoring ceased, and I heard a loud, "What the d—l is all this row?" The enquiry made no impression on me, for I did not abate one jot of my energy till I had completed my toilet and departed, making as much noise as if I had fallen down two flights of stairs. Before I left the hotel I had an interview with the landlord, to whom I related what had happened. In the morning a complaint was duly lodged, and I believe he gave some wholesome advice as to how young men should behave when resident in hotels, where there are other guests equally deserving of consideration.

For one who had to pass so much time in hotels I was very unfortunate in being a light sleeper. Even the rattling of a mouse behind a skirting would disturb me. But cock-crowing was my supreme grievance. I generally contrived to get a bedroom as far removed from the poultry yard as possible; but in the tourist season I had just to make the best of what accommodation was offered. One would imagine that in a seaside inn there would be no disturbing sounds during the night. This, however, is by no means the case. One summer I had occasion to stay for a week in the small but very comfortable hotel at Scarinish in Tiree. The weather was delightfully warm and sunny. Unfortunately for me there happened to be an unusual number of visitors, and all the available bedrooms in the hotel were engaged. Thinking of perfect quietness, I was not sorry when I was relegated to a newly built small wooden annex, which had been fitted up as a bedroom, to be used when no other sleeping apartment was available. But I soon found I was very far from being away from noise. Certainly there was no cock-crowing, but in the very early morning the vagrant ewes with their hungry lambs came round, and their baaing was heart-breaking. They had hardly passed into the distance when the ducks in search of slugs came quacking along. Meantime a calf, for reasons known only to himself, kept rubbing his hindquarters against the door. Above all rose the incessant cackle of sea-gulls and other aquatic birds hunting for food at the ebb tide. Sleep was impossible. I laid my grievance before the sympathetic hostess, who kindly contrived to effect a change. As a fact, I got the bedroom of a young chap who boasted that an earthquake would not disturb him.

As might be expected, few hotels where food is plentiful are without rats. The disturbance created by these pests I never could endure. It was my misfortune to have to stay in a Perthshire hotel which was particularly infested with them. I had to visit evening classes in the district in the winter time. When all was still I was frequently disturbed by hearing the rodents scurrying about the bedroom floor. One night one of them almost ran across my face as I lay awake. This I deemed too much liberty. Sleep was out of the question. Although the night was bitterly cold, I sprang out of bed and struck a light. What my sleepy eyes beheld proved that I was not a moment too soon, for there at the left-hand corner of the grate, where there was a considerable aperture, I saw one of my stockings being tugged inside. Needless to say, my activity was prompt. I was just in time to retrieve it. Afterwards, I never spent a night in that hotel without placing my clothes, and particularly my stockings, beyond the reach of these unscrupulous thieves.

Let me record another episode connected with the rat species. For the reason stated above, I had to put up in another Perthshire hotel, where I was relegated to a bedroom at the angle of two long corridors with bedrooms on each side. I had hardly fallen asleep when an energetic rodent commenced to scurry up the wall beside me and then across the ceiling. He kept on doing this every minute till I concluded he was doing a round for exercise. Knowing that the hotel was without tourists at that time, I took it for granted that there would be plenty of empty rooms quite near. Accordingly, I determined to shift my quarters and seek repose elsewhere. Rising, I lit my candle, quietly opened the door, and proceeded barefooted along the corridor in quest of a room with an open door, which would be almost certain to be unoccupied. I soon found one which looked promising. To make certain that there was no sleeper inside, with my forefinger I silently pushed open the door far enough to admit the candlestick. Hoping that the sudden illumination would awaken the sleeper, if there chanced to be one, I paused. There was no sound, so I entered, took possession of the bed, and soon fell sound asleep. In the morning I was roused by the persistent knocking of the 'boots' on the door of the room I had vacated. His face when he saw me and heard me shouting "All right!" from the far end of the corridor would have done credit to a tragical type of film. All the same, when I meditated on the incident on my homeward journey I realised that my action was rather risky, for had the room been occupied by a lady fond of fresh air, no cock-and-bull story about rats would have availed to save me from ignominy.

The following incident illustrates what presence of mind and ingenuity can effect in an awkward situation. Along with the local doctor I had been spending the evening in a manse, where we were so hospitably entertained that we did not think of taking our departure till well after midnight. By this time all the doors of the hotel where I was staying were shut and locked. Hammer as we might on every likely door, we failed to rouse the hotel porter. After a little cogitation, however, my companion contrived to bring him to his feet. Seizing the large barrow by which visitors' luggage was conveyed to the station, he commenced to wheel it backwards and forwards below the window of the porter's sleeping-place. Instantly the window flew up. A head appeared and an angry voice demanded who had the daring to steal the barrow. Sharp words, which it were better to omit, passed. I was soon admitted, and the doctor took his departure, congratulating himself on having done one good turn to a belated Inspector.

Early in my inspectorial career I was under the necessity of having to pass a night at a small wayside inn in one of the larger islands of the Outer Hebrides. Here I was told beforehand sleepers were not catered for. The landlord derived his living from the cultivation of a croft and the sale of spirituous liquor to wayfarers. He was a widower with the reputation of being 'a bit of a character.' Being fore-warned, I was prepared for some exhibition of his eccentricity. I arrived in the evening, and, entering the open door, was confronted by mine host himself. To my surprise, on learning who I was, he assumed an affable, almost familiar air, and even condescended to ask what he could do to oblige me. In a grateful tone I enquired if he could let me have a room for the night. "Certainly, certainly!" he said, and, turning round, he shouted, "Here, Morag, show this gentleman up to Number 7." The buxom Morag promptly appeared, and, muttering in Gaelic what I concluded was, "This way, sir," she preceded me up a very creaky, loose-jointed staircase. Close to the top she opened a door having a broken panel, and showed me into an evil-smelling garret with a sloping ceiling on each side. It was lighted by a small single pane roof light covered with cobwebs, which indicated that fresh air was not considered essential. Along one side was a wooden arrangement forming two bedsteads, end to end. But, tell it not in Gath, there was only one corresponding den in the whole inn. From what I had heard of the landlord, I was not in the least surprised that he dubbed my apartment Number 7. I went downstairs, and, being hungry, I did ample justice to the good ham and fresh eggs with boiled tea which Morag got ready with an expedition that quite surprised me. As I ate, my attention was sometimes distracted by an occasional fowl which strutted about the floor in search of crumbs. How I passed the hours of twilight I am not quite certain. Probably I spent the time strolling by the 'sad sea waves' meditating on the problem of life in these outlandish parts. It grew dark, and as there seemed to be no hope of peaceful seclusion in the small apartment on the ground floor, I betook myself at an unusually early hour to Number 7. I had a feeling that the landlord was rather disappointed that I did not sample his *usquebaugh* before I retired. However, he made no suggestion as to the propriety of imbibing the proverbial 'night cap.' He lit my candle, and wished me a sound sleep as I pounded my way upstairs to my appointed lair. Having shut and barred the door with a movable bolt on the inside, I got into the more distant of the two beds. Later, while I was dozing, and far from feeling comfortable, I heard the arrival of a man, who I afterwards learned was a peripatetic tea traveller. The hilarious welcome he received convinced me that he and the landlord were old friends. As I lay listening, I was satisfied that two convivial souls — *Arcades ambo* — were enjoying themselves to the full in the parlour I had vacated. In due time the merrymaking came to an end, when, to my consternation, I heard the bagman ascending the stairs with so much noise that I had no hesitation in concluding that he was in a state of inebriety. The landlord evidently preceded him, for it was he who, finding the door bolted, began to hammer upon it, at the same time shouting for admission. By the dim light from the candle which he held in his hand, I could just discern his angry face as he peered through the broken panel. But I was determined to admit no one, more particularly a bagman who appeared to be far from sober. I lay without word or movement. I think I even snored loudly to camouflage my obstinacy. At last, finding the effort to get admission hopeless, with no end of muttered objurgations they retraced their steps, much to my relief. Where the bagman slept I know not. Nor did I make enquiry. In all likelihood he and the landlord shared the same bed. Neither of them was in evidence in the morning when I paid Morag the 'lawin' and quietly departed, never again to spend a night in that wretched hostelry.

Another inn to which I sometimes gave a wide berth occurs to me. It likewise was situated in a Hebridean island. Circumstances over which she had no control prevented the delicate landlady from giving the requisite attention to visitors. The result was that cleanliness was non-existent, nor was the food always satisfactory. I arrived one afternoon, and was conducted to the bedroom I was to occupy. In the bed lay a man, who, if I remember rightly, was a shepherd. He was sound asleep. A very strong aroma of whisky pervaded the apartment. The landlady, not in the least perturbed, kindly assured me he had been feeling unwell, and that he would be sure to vacate the bed before I required it. For this information I was grateful, for I had no desire to share it with him. It was out of consideration for her worried appearance that I refrained from expressing a hope that the sheets would be changed. As the night closed in and the mists were beginning to blanket the surrounding mountains, having no congenial work on hand, I betook myself to bed. Well do I remember pushing my way through screeching fowls as I mounted the staircase to find the bed occupied by the pet lamb. Needless to say, I evicted the fleecy tenant without ceremony, and, shoving him downstairs, shut and bolted the door. Though the bed was delightfully warm, I cannot say that my sleep was of the soundest, even in that remote glen, where the sound of falling waters and the sough of the wind, blowing fresh from the western seas, might have been expected to exercise a soporific effect.

One, travelling year in year out in the Highlands, half a century ago, got accustomed to unusual experiences and extraordinary make-shifts. The sights one saw in connection with strangers were often most amusing, as when the Londoner, who had never been to Scotland before, appeared in a brand new tartan kilt, sporran and *skean dhu*, which latter he was doubtless soon surprised to find more ornamental than useful. It was only then that he realised that the land was not full of wild caterans and big, black-bearded smugglers. In London he had seen the soldiers of a Highland regiment all arrayed in kilts. That settled it. In Scotland he must wear what the Scots wear. His astonishment must often have been great when on reaching Inverness he saw nobody in the garb of Old Gaul save an occasional Highland laird, the scion of some clan, whose ancestors had worn no other dress from time immemorial, and who were probably responsible for no end of stirring Scottish history.

I was standing on the south platform of Dingwall railway station one night in the height of the tourist season. Beside me was a Church of England curate, who had come to Scotland for the first time. He was bound for Strathpeffer to assist my brother, who was Dean of the Diocese. On the opposite platform, waiting the arrival of the south-going mail, was one Theodore Napier, conspicuously arrayed in the full dress of a gentleman Highlander of the time of Prince Charlie. The curate, whose eye was naturally attracted by the 'apparition,' suddenly broke off our conversation with, "What's that?" When I replied that *it* was a native of Australia or New Zealand, which was quite true, he promptly asked, "Is he a Maori?" The arrival of his train prevented me from making explanations, but I am convinced that my young friend, a graduate of Oxford University, all the way to his destination was turning over in his mind how very far he had been misled in his conception of the habiliments of the New Zealand aborigines.

When on duty in Sutherland I had oftener than once to sojourn at a country inn much frequented by anglers in the River Oykell. I arrived rather late one evening, and was informed by the innkeeper's wife that a garret at the top of the house was the only available sleeping apartment. This was no new experience when Walton's disciples were in force. Before accepting her offer, however, I made a point of seeing the room. It was a long, narrow apartment with a sloping ceiling, which sectionally gave it a triangular appearance. It was lighted by a small roof light, which I was pleased to see was open. The bed was, as it were, slipped into the tunnel-like end. My looks must have betrayed my thoughts, for before I could express dissatisfaction she blurted out that John Bright, in his day a keen angler, had slept in that bed for more than a month. This was history indeed. I was satisfied. What a Cabinet Minister could put up with it would ill become a humble member of the inspectorate to cavil at. That night before falling asleep I lay conning over in my mind all I had ever heard or read of this son of a Lancashire cotton spinner who took an active part in the Free Trade agitation and ultimately became President of the Board of Trade. I fell asleep and, like John Bunyan, I dreamed. In the morning while dressing I could not help imagining I saw corpulent John Bright donning his fishing garb in that cramped apartment.

It was in a large tourist hotel in the West Highlands that I happened one evening to stroll into the billiard-room, when the table was in possession of two professionals, in whose play the other visitors seated around were evidently deeply interested. The game being finished, the winner was bragging of his having once nearly beaten the champion, Roberts, when a waiter entered, and with a bow that would have done credit to Uriah Heep, presented him with his bill on a small silver tray. At once scrutinising it, the boaster exclaimed, "A shilling for a bath! Look here, I have not had a bath for six months," an assertion which his incredulous hearers generously attributed to his wrath at being seemingly taken in. "Then it's high time you had one," said the cool Irish waiter. That this was adding insult to injury the visitor's subsequent language attested. In the end, however, that shilling was deleted, and probably transferred to another tourist's account.

I was never enamoured of hotels where cards bearing Scripture texts were the chief decoration of the bedroom walls. I sometimes doubted if these, as well as the large print New Testaments so common on the dressing-tables, were placed there at the hotel-keeper's expense. I was fain to think that some kindly soul had distributed them to soothe those harassed with extortionate hotel bills. Let me quote a few of the texts. 'God bless our home.' Well, he would be cruel indeed who would say nay to that. 'The soul that sinneth it shall die,' would be poor consolation to the one who had been imbibing too freely before going to bed, if he was able to read it. 'The Sabbath was made for man and not man for the Sabbath.' This was most appropriate in Highland inns, but it takes a clear brain to follow the reasoning. 'A house divided against itself cannot stand.' This conveys a warning to the individual who, having quarrelled with his better half, sought refuge in the Highlands till the embers of strife had died down. 'Why are ye fearful. O ye of little faith?' would be very soothing to one whom dread of a stiff bill on the morrow kept from sleeping soundly. 'Watch and pray' was excellent advice to the guest to keep a sharp eye on what he ate and to pray that his bill might at least be reasonable.

In the tourist season hotel-keepers argued that as their season was short they had to lay on the charges 'while the sun shone.' Nor were they inclined to deal leniently with the School Inspector whose expenses they suspected came out of the national purse. But after all was said and done, it was rather galling to be charged at tourist rates when one might reasonably look for the privileges to which a regular visitor is entitled. However, some men acted honourably. The hotel-keeper at Balmacarra I unhesitatingly place in this category. One year he charged me on the tourist scale. At my next annual visit he apologised and like a gentleman refunded the overcharge. Sad to say, he did not live long.

The following lines I composed one evening when sauntering in the neighbourhood of a tourist hotel, where the charges fully exhausted my night's allowance:

A HIELAN' HOTEL
Here's nestlin' in a cosy neuk,
A bricht spot on the cheek o' natur',
Where heathery braes its lums o'erlook
A braw hotel's attractive featur'.
There's feedin' here for ilka beast
That hungry gangs within its steadin';
For folk, guid faith! there's sic a feast
As weel micht sair a Royal weddin'.
But tak' ye tent, gin ye come here,
To hae yer purse wi' siller packit;
For, tho' there's routh o' halesome cheer,
Sma' mercies soon will lichter mak' it.

Chapter XVI

RECREATIONS

Sportsmen rejoice when the season comes round when they can indulge in their favourite sport. As Dryden says:

The face lights up when gloomy winter flees,
And sports we love once more return to please.

'All work and no play makes Jack a dull boy' is trite, but it is nevertheless true. The chief recreation of the bulk of School Inspectors is golf. I have heard it said that inspecting schools is the Inspector's function and playing 'gowff' his duty: one might also add 'his hobby.' Certainly, in their company one hears more about the royal and ancient game than about the general progress of education. But while golf did not appeal to me, angling, which Walton described as 'the most calm, quiet and innocent form of recreation,' always did. When inspecting schools in Lewis over forty years ago the district Inspector and I on our rounds almost invariably carried our fishing equipment with us. The kindly factor gave us full liberty to fish on all the lochs and streams, except the rivers Creed and Grimersta, which were always well let. Our favourite loch lay near the Garrynahine road about six miles from Stornoway. I forget its name, but that is immaterial. Here on our way home from a school we used to call a halt, dismiss our wagonette, and betake ourselves to the loch where we fished, each doing the whole round, before

The western waves of ebbing day
Rolled o'er the moors *their level way.*

Then with well-filled creels of beautiful trout we trudged home to Stornoway, inhaling the clean, fresh sea breeze that for ever sweeps the melancholy wastes of peat and heather characteristic of this the largest of the Outer Hebrides.

At Barvas, on the west side of Lewis, I once saw what a naturalist would deem worth recording. It was on a calm, sultry evening as it was getting dark that I was standing amongst some tall, damp grass and rushes, engaged in fishing near the mouth of the Barvas river. Suddenly I detected a curious commotion about my feet. On investigating the cause I was surprised to see that eels of various sizes had left the stagnant pools and were wriggling their way through the moist grass to other similar pools. It was the first and only time I have ever seen this extraordinary migration of eels.

The Inspector of the district and I were often lucky in enjoying fishing on preserved water. At the last meeting for the year of the School Board of Kilmallie, over which the late Lord Abinger presided, he very considerably made a point of instructing his factor not to omit to give my chief and me a day's fishing on Mucomir pool near Spean Bridge. This had the reputation of being one of the finest salmon stretches in the country. No doubt it still maintains this honour. Unfortunately for us, our annual visit to the district was generally rather early in the season. Though there was always the chance of getting a clean run fish, 'kelts,' or unclean ones, abounded and readily took the fly. Of course, they had invariably to be promptly committed to the water by the attendant keepers. However, we sometimes managed to land a clean fish or two in the course of the day. This we found compensation for the wearisome task of landing numerous lean-looking specimens.

On the river Garry, which flows into Loch Oich in Inverness-shire, we generally spent an afternoon and evening fishing for salmon after concluding our professional duties for the day. This river stands high in the estimation of anglers, and in those days it was always well let. However, the Inspectors were considered men of some importance, and that they might have a good time while in the neighbourhood of Invergarry the lessee very considerately refrained from fishing himself, and placed the river at our disposal. His kindness was exceptional. One year, when luck was against us, as we passed the hotel in which he resided, our wagonette was stopped, and two fine salmon carefully wrapped in rushes handed up to us. A more generous act could hardly be conceived. It was greatly appreciated and never forgotten. I may add that in Father Col, the aged priest at Fort Augustus, I had a good friend who, in his youth a keen disciple of Izaak, was always willing to overhaul my book in the selection of suitable flies for this particular river. It was with him that I visited the chapel attached to the monastery at Fort Augustus to see the ceremony of creating Sir Hunter Blair a monk. As we walked down the avenue after the function I said, "Well,

Father Col, what do you think of what you have seen?" "I think very little of him," he promptly replied. "It would set him better to stay at home and be a good Catholic and kind to his tenants." "And who was that old Bishop who took such an active part in the ceremony?" was my next question. "Och! that was Johnny Mac—, the Bishop of—. I was at college with him; but I would need to call him My Lord now." As part of the reason why he belittled the whole affair I should add that he had no love for the monks, whom he regarded as interlopers poaching, as he said, in his special sphere of labour. He was a kindly soul and lived to a ripe old age. R.I.P.

Writing of Fort Augustus, I remember an exciting fishing adventure in that neighbourhood. In the 'eighties of last century a very well known and genial officer of Excise was stationed there. He was a keen sportsman, and alleged that he had got permission from a proprietor, whose land bordered on the west side, to fish for salmon on Loch Ness. He maintained, with what legal justification I know not, that this allowed him to fish anywhere and everywhere on the loch. A case was pending in court when the district Inspector and I were on official duty in the neighbourhood. As we were loafing about after our day's work, he invited us to accompany him in his boat to the east side of the loch, where on a promising stretch we could troll for salmon with minnow or spoon bait. We rose to the occasion, and in course of time secured a fine specimen weighing over twenty pounds. With this trophy we rowed back to the pier near our friend's house. Here we landed, to our great relief unchallenged. With a view to concealing the salmon I passed the cotton cover of my rod through the gills, so that when knotted it formed a loop. This I slung over my head, the fish depending from my neck in front of me. Over it I buttoned my long, big, heavy ulster. It was difficult walking even the short distance between the pier and the officer's house, but I hobbled along and finally reached it after considerable effort. His wife admitted me. Ignorant of the unique burden I bore, she asked me to go upstairs, as she had company in the ground floor parlour. I knew I was risking a great deal when I essayed to mount the stairs. At every step the salmon's flat tail would get in my way. I had the sensation of treading on ice. A 'tragedy' was inevitable. When I was half way up, the strain caused the knot to slip, with the result that the fish, tail first, shot through my legs and down the steps at express speed. Had the lady, who was following me to show the room, not quickly clutched the stair railing she would certainly have been upset, with consequences it baffles me to contemplate. Her fright was naturally great. Her exclamation I refrain from recording. We afterwards gathered that gamekeepers had been watching us through field-glasses. Not expecting our return so soon, they had left the landing-place for their evening meal, and were absent at the very time we came ashore. Had they met us I doubt the dignity of the inspectorate would have suffered.

But, though I had often the privilege of fishing for salmon, I had oftener the opportunity of testing my skill with sea trout. I must admit that in my experience a sea trout of the size of a small grilse gives excitement that cannot be equalled in any other form of fresh water fishing.

One year while I was sojourning at Torridon House the number of guests happened to be large. The weather was inclined to be wet, hence most of them were loafing indoors. It was on a Saturday afternoon that my hostess, having seen me arrive armed with fishing equipment, joined her husband in approaching me with a request that, as she had such a large house party to cater for, I might oblige her by going a-fishing for sea trout in the river that traversed Glen Torridon. Most anglers would have been only too delighted to accede to her request. But not being too well supplied with changes of clothes, I was anything but willing to risk being drenched to the skin. When it did rain in that quarter it simply fell in bucketfuls. I knew this, and could not help blurting out some reference to the unpropitious appearance of the weather. Her husband, however, did not see eye to eye with me on this point, so he ultimately said, "Come along with me to the ghillies' room downstairs. Let's get their opinion.' I followed him sullenly. In an apartment in the basement stood four or five stalwart Highlanders. My host asked a big man with a white beard, who was the head keeper, if he thought there was any likelihood of my catching sea trout in the river. To my intense delight, casting a glance towards the window, with a shrug of his shoulder he replied, "Ach! no, Sir, I don't think he would get any fush to-night." By his side stood a smallish, well-knit fellow to whom he next appealed with a "What do you say, Angus?" Whether Angus foresaw a handsome *pour boire* or not I cannot say, but to my great disappointment he replied, "Ach! I believe he would be getting some fush." That settled it. Nothing more was said. The coachman was rung up, and at the shortest notice a dogcart was at the door. As if *pour encourager le pêcheur*, my host, whether in jest or earnest, suggested that as I was going to the deer country I might as well take a rifle, so that if I got no fish I might be lucky enough to get a stag. He also added facetiously that one would be enough, and if a Royal so much the better. With a forced smile I refused the rifle and stuck to the rod. Off we set. I sat beside the liveried coachman, while Angus, clutching the fishing material, occupied the back seat. We drove to a point more than three miles up the glen. The farther we went the more gloomy the atmosphere became, and my spirits sank in proportion. At last we dismounted, and the coachman returned home. Little conversation passed between me and Angus as he led me through the rank heather to the bank of the river, which appeared to be much swollen by rain that must have been falling far off amongst the mountains. After he had rigged up the rod and donned a fly, which he took an unconscionable time to select, I got to work, I had hardly commenced, however, when the rain, as I expected, came down in torrents. Silently and dejectedly I kept on casting for fully half an hour, but without getting a single bite. Exasperation took possession of me when I felt the wet reaching my skin. In a temper I tossed the rod on the bank, and with a peremptory "Come on home, Angus, I am not going to fish any longer," I bent my steps through the wet heather in a beeline for the road. Angus in a reticent mood reeled in the line, but did not dismantle the rod. Instead, he laid it over his shoulder and followed at a respectful distance. Once more on the road we proceeded in Indian file, my companion leading. Without exchanging a word we plodded homewards for about two miles, when Angus suddenly stopped, and shouting, "Come down and try this pool, Sir," began to wade through the heather to a point about one hundred yards from the road. He gave me no opportunity of declining the invitation. I knew he was keeping his eye on the river as we came along. In no good frame of mind I followed him. The spot where we halted was a bend or elbow of the river, where frequent spates had washed away the soil, leaving a deep pool flanked by a steep bank. Once more with a medium-sized 'Jock Scot' on the cast I commenced to whip the turbulent muddy stream. But, ye gods! what sport! The pool was simply swarming with sea trout resting on their way up from the sea, as was evidenced by the sea lice still adhering to their backs. Suffice it to say that for the next hour one beautiful fish was hardly landed when another was on. When I grew tired, for a strong greenheart rod needs some muscle, Angus took up the sport. This went on till the basket was full, and as many as it could carry strung by the gills on to the rod cover. Thus laden, we concluded that it was time we were making for Torridon House, where dinner was at 7 p.m. When we reached the head keeper's cottage, which happened to be by the roadside, Angus, struggling under his silvery load and the fishing tackle, begged permission to interview him as to work for Monday. Well did I know that this was only a lame excuse for an opportunity of proving to his superior that his prognostications with regard to weather suitable for fishing were not always to be depended on. Though I was not within hearing, I could gather from their gestures that their conversation was particularly animated. Nor had I any dubiety regarding the theme. By this time, in our fatigued and drenched condition, I deemed refreshment desirable, if only it could be got. Although I knew quite well that my host abhorred spirituous liquor, I ventured to ask Angus where a 'drop' might be obtained. After some misgiving, which I soon allayed by assurance of secrecy, he led me to the cottage of an old woman, to whom he explained our plight in most forceful Gaelic. The result was that the *cailleach*, risking eviction, supplied us to satiety out of a small pig jar with the rawest of smuggled whisky clear as crystal. My small share I liberally diluted with water, but, adhering to the custom of his ancestors, Angus gulped down a half cupful of the vile, fiery liquid with the usual announcement, "I will be taking the water afterwards." But, like his forebears, he never did take it. When I reached Torridon House everybody became so engrossed in the contemplation of my afternoon's catch that I verily believe, had I been soaked in whisky from head to foot, not a soul would have concerned himself about the aroma, and, if he did, would have had the good sense to overlook it.

One year at Knoydart as the guest of the Bairds, to whom the estate then belonged, I had a somewhat alarming adventure. I happened to be fishing alone for salmon on the river Dessary. Accompanying me was a large deer-hound that for some unaccountable reason had taken a fancy to me. The stream at one point flows through peculiar strata, for the most part consisting of friable rock full of very tiny crimson-coloured grains of sand. I pocketed a quantity, for I had never seen anything like it before. This I afterwards showed to a geologist, who confirmed my opinion that it consisted of garnets, so minute, however, that they were of no commercial value. But to the fishing: I kept casting for about an hour without success. As it was nearing the dinner hour, I commenced to reel in my line. I had hardly begun when the hound, that had been keeping close to my heels all the time, made a vicious snap at my legs. This appeared to be his method of showing his displeasure when I gave up fishing. The situation was certainly alarming. However, I managed to remove the fly, and, pretending to be fishing, I leisurely retraced my steps till I reached an opening of a path leading through a corn field straight up to the mansion. Into this I sprang, and hurried along without glancing behind to see if my assailant was following. I afterwards learned that the hound was particularly fond of fishers, whom he took every opportunity of accompanying.

Fishing is allowed to be one of the most fascinating of sports. To me, the opportunities so abundant in the 'eighties of last century were always anticipated with the acme of pleasure. If the basket was not always full, in surroundings dear to an artistic heart, I must admit 'I preferr'd my pleasure to my gains.'

Chapter XVII

PERSONALIA

P assing so much time in hotels and private houses, I was brought into contact with a great many interesting persons. One year while at Tongue, in the north of Sutherlandshire, I forgathered with Thomas Faed, the well-known artist. In appearance, he was typically of the Victorian era. He had fine, clean-cut features, enhanced by long Dundreary whiskers. He invariably wore a red tie. Although he had come equipped with painting materials, he evidently found the lochs in that quarter too tempting, for he devoted his whole time to fishing, to the neglect of the brush. We often had a pleasant discussion on Art, but he was more inclined to talk of his favourite sport than about pictures. Several anglers were in the hotel at that time. One night I overheard a long discussion between the artist and another fisher on the merits of Loch Laoghal, some six miles distant. The result was that the latter, accompanied by a reliable ghillie, set off for this fine sheet of water at six o'clock next morning. Everybody was surprised when the two returned to the hotel in the early afternoon without any fish. The explanation was that when they reached the loch the angler found to his extreme wrath and vexation that his guide had left the fly-book at the hotel. Accordingly, there was nothing for it but a retracing of steps. To account for the long time taken to do so, the angler said, "I just took him to the top of Ben Laoghal to improve his memory." Now, this mountain, one of the finest in Scotland, is about 2504 feet high, and as the day was warm, with midges and other bloodsucking insects abundant, there is every probability that the drastic step proved successful.

William Black, the novelist, was another keen disciple of Izaak. My association with him was not of the happiest. One day as he was fishing from a boat on the river Ness I happened to be walking along the bank accompanied by a small water spaniel belonging to a friend with whom I had just had lunch. Naturally, the animal went in for a bath. It no sooner did so than I was startled to hear a shrill voice on the other side loudly protesting against the intrusion of my canine friend in his happy hunting-ground. Undismayed, I waited till he rowed across and peremptorily demanded that I should take the dog out of the water. This at first I refused to do, at the same time pointing out that the animal was only obeying its natural instinct. I told him I did know something about fishing, and that any commotion made by the dog on my side of the river would not disturb the fish on the other side where he was plying the rod. We were both a little heated, but as I had no desire to be offensive, much less disobliging, I pursued my way with the dog on the leash.

Writing of Black brings to my mind an incident connected with his novel *A Princess of Thule*, the scene of which is laid in Lewis. Sheila, as everybody knows who has read the tale, is the heroine. The wife of a schoolmaster in the parish of Uig told me that one day whilst she and some girl companions were at play in front of the Post Office Mr.

Black and a friend approached. The former noted her beautiful golden hair, and laying his hand on her head, he asked her name. On her replying that it was Sheila, she said he turned to his friend with the remark, "What a pretty name." Although the name was by no means uncommon in the Highlands, from this incident she concluded that the novelist then heard it for the first time, and, being charmed with it, gave it to the Highland peat-loving lassie of his novel.

Another interesting gentleman I sometimes met at Creagory Hotel in Benbecula was Dr. Carment, S.S.C., of Edinburgh. He was a keen angler, and devoted much time to the sport. On Sundays, acting on his convictions, he took special interest in religious matters. I was sitting alone one Saturday forenoon revising examination papers, when a hand, passed over my shoulder from behind, deposited a large chunk of cake on the table before me. I turned round to find Mrs. Carment beaming with smiles. On my soliciting an explanation of this unexpected gift, she said, "This is John's birthday." I am afraid I was rather indiscreet when on the spur of the moment I asked his age. However, she seemed to take it not amiss, for she at once said, "He is just seventy-two to-day." She was a most kindly lady, and everybody loved her.

An awkward little episode occurred one summer on board the steamer plying between Stornoway and Loch Carron. The district Inspector and I were travelling during the night, and as all the berths had been engaged, we had perforce to take up our quarters on the space reserved for luggage in the after part of the cabin. Taking advantage of my being a light sleeper, my companion bade me rouse him in the early morning when we were nearing Portree. About seven o'clock I got up and, only half awake, roughly shook the shoulder of a fair-haired young man lying not far from me. His face was turned away so that I could not see it. Glancing up, he asked with curled brows what was the matter. I bade him bestir himself as we were nearing Portree. With that I left him and went on deck, where I paced backwards and forwards, thinking of the sailors who were busy swabbing the decks. The air was delightfully fresh and cool. In a short time I noticed the young man whom I took to be the Inspector standing on deck at the door leading to the cabin stair. I now realised that I had wakened the wrong man. To rectify my mistake I hurried downstairs past him without remark or apology. He seemed to take no notice of me. On regaining the deck I observed that the sailors when passing him lifted their caps and showed signs of obsequiousness. On enquiring who he was, I was rather surprised to learn that he was Lord Fincastle, son and heir of the Earl of Dunmore, who was also a passenger. Satisfied that he would benefit by the balmy sea air of the early morning, I did not trouble to apologise for having wakened him so unceremoniously. Thus the morning passed with comedy; but tragedy was to follow.

After leaving Portree 'a stiff breeze blew: the white foam flew,' and some passengers were sea-sick. When off the small island of Scalpay we saw a boat being rowed towards the steamer. On board were two men and three women, forming a load much greater than such a small craft could carry in a rough sea. The women were servants, who had been left behind when the owner quitted the island for the season. They were now on their way south. The men were likewise employees on the estate. They were rowing the women out to put them on board the steamer for Strome Ferry, at that time the railway terminus. For some reason difficult of explanation they brought the boat to the wrong side, despite the shouted warnings of both the Captain and seamen. One man, rising in the bow, seized the rope that was thrown to him. Instantly that end of the boat dipped, and the on-coming wave almost filled it. Another wave followed, with the result that the boat sank and floated away, leaving the occupants struggling in the water. The man who clutched the rope retained his grasp, and was hauled on board. His companion went under, but reappeared. I saw the Captain swing himself over the side of the steamer and stretch out his foot, hoping that he might see and seize it. But all I noticed was an open hand that came near the surface and then disappeared. The young lad sank to rise no more. A boat was swiftly launched, and happily all the half-drowned females were rescued. As bad luck would have it, the lad was an only son, and the sole support of his widowed mother. This becoming known, while excitement was at its height and sympathy in the ascendant, Lord Dunmore, with commendable presence of mind, passed his cap round for subscriptions for behoof of the unfortunate lad's mother. In the circumstances a handsome sum was collected before the steamer reached Strome Ferry. In the following year I was on board the same steamer on the same day of the month and at the same spot, when the purser informed me that there were six persons on board who had been witnesses of that accident. Pointing to a lonely-looking girl with a meditative face sitting on a coil of ropes at the stern, he added, "And that's one of the women who were in the water."

A very energetic lady who made her appearance in the Hebrides every year was Miss Rainy, sister of Principal Rainy of the Free Church College, Edinburgh. Certain small schools for which certificated teachers were not necessary were taught between sessions by divinity students. In these Miss Rainy evinced a special interest, and seized every opportunity that offered to accompany the Inspector when he went to examine the schools. At the same time, I am not sure that the young men were always grateful for her presence. In the presence of strangers children in a small school are apt to be shy, and cannot be expected to show to advantage.

Within my recollection a unique case occurred while a school in the neighbourhood of Balmoral was being examined. The door opened and Queen Victoria entered. The presence of Royalty would have been disconcerting to most Inspectors, but fortunately on this occasion the Inspector happened to be an exceptionally able and self-possessed member of the profession. He proved himself equal to the somewhat trying circumstances. But, though endowed with a coolness almost amounting to stoicism, he privately admitted to me that he had no desire a second time to examine a school in presence of the Sovereign of the Realm.

I once spent a week-end in North Uist in the home of a very cultured lady, sister of the factor to Sir John Orde.

The house was situated at a point looking northwards towards the island of Bernera in the Sound of Harris. What specially charmed me was her knowledge of antiquarian lore. After a gale on the beautiful white sands by the seashore, she had picked up a marvellous collection of bone implements and other articles of great interest and value. I have often wondered what became of them. It was rare to come across such a fine private collection. It was when inspecting the school on Bernera, where there is no pier or landing-place, that I had to be carried ashore across the shoals on the back of a sturdy bare-legged native. So far as I recollect, this was the only occasion on which I had to undergo such an experience.

Another individual who showed justifiable pride in his collection of curios was Walter Dennison, with whom I forgathered in the island of Sanday, in Orkney. He took me over his house and showed me his private museum, containing, amongst other things, a stuffed specimen of every bird that had been captured in Orkney. In one case I saw a hoopoe, which, like the humming bird alongside of it, he explained had probably been borne on a gale to these remote islands. As I examined the collection I became almost sceptical of my being at that moment in Orkney. But besides these he had many things to which he attached great importance. One that afforded me special delight to handle was a long nautical telescope such as is used by sea Captains. He assured me that it was the very glass that belonged to Gow, the notorious pirate who commanded the *George*, a vessel of 200 tons, armed with 18 guns, in which he sailed from the Barbary Coast in 1725. The sloop ultimately ran aground in the Calf Sound of Eday, when an ancestor of his came into possession of the telescope. As I looked seawards through it I wondered if it was possible that Sir Walter Scott, who is said to have based his tale of *The Pirate* on what he gathered of this notorious sea robber, ever had an opportunity of placing his eye at the end of this same instrument. Mr. Dennison was an author of some repute, and had also a fine library of books connected with Orkney. Altogether the contents of his house was to me an eye-opener.

Coll was one of the islands visited by Dr. Johnson on his memorable tour. Here he was hospitably entertained by the then Chieftain. Viewing the weed-covered remnant of an ancient pier in front of the hotel, I felt sure that it must have been in existence in his day, and was more than likely the very spot where he and James Boswell first set foot on the island. Discussing this with the local factor, a very intelligent man, I made a discovery. He led me to an outhouse where things which had done service in their day in the proprietor's mansion were stored. Here he produced two mahogany bedposts of long, spiral shape, carefully roped together and labelled. These, he said, were two of the posts belonging to the bed in which Johnson slept—all that was rescued when the furniture was being overhauled.

I am convinced Coll could have furnished another curio, which would have deemed worthy of a place in an antiquarian museum, had steps been taken to preserve it. Though it may not come under the heading of this chapter, the incident may for convenience be recorded here.

The school of Acha is situated in the southern portion

of the island not far from the laird's mansion, near which is the ruin of the old Castle of Breakacha, one of the most complete I ever set eyes on, and a standing monument of the days when might was right. This school was taught by a lady whose husband had to give up teaching on account of deafness. He spent some time cutting peats in a fine deep bank near the schoolhouse. Being a man of superior intelligence, he kept his eyes open for anything interesting in the peat formation. After I had lunched in the schoolhouse, he produced a piece of oak about two feet long and nearly a foot in breadth which he found more than eight feet below the surface of the peat bank, where there was no trace of wood of any kind. It was scooped out lengthwise and soaking wet. I examined it very carefully, and, taking everything into account, came to the conclusion that it was a child's toy boat of the Stone Age. I am of the same opinion still. As I handed it back to him he carelessly dropped it, with the result that it broke in pieces brittle as china. When I visited the school in the following year, on my enquiring what had become of the fragments, he drew my attention to a piece of shrivelled, sun-baked oak lying on top of the garden wall, all that remained of what, had it found a place in an antiquarian museum and been suspended in water, would, I feel certain, have been one of the most unique and interesting specimens in the collection. I may add that he presented me with a number of hazel nuts with kernels intact which he found in peat many feet below the surface. The island is devoid of trees, but as on other wind-swept Hebridean isles, roots of what must ages ago have been huge forest trees are often found embedded in peat banks.

Here is an incident which may interest some of my readers. One year when at Torridon, Mr. Darroch, the laird, and I happened to be walking along the road on the south side of the loch, when we saw approaching a wagonette drawn by a pair of horses. He recognised the conveyance, and bade me take a look of the gentleman who was probably in it. As it passed I saw an old man with whom my companion exchanged salutations. "Who is he?" I asked. "That," said he, "is the Earl of Lovelace, who married Ada, Lord Byron's daughter." Of her he wrote in *Childe Harold's Pilgrimage:*

Is thy face like thy mother's, my fair child,
Ada, sole daughter of my house and heart?
When last I saw thy young blue eyes they smiled
And then we parted—not as now we part,
But with a hope, etc.

Seeing the Earl, I felt I had got hold of an interesting link with one of the great poets of the early Victorian era, and I was glad that I had done so. At that time he was proprietor of Ben Damph deer forest.

I once had another interesting individual pointed out to me in North Uist. The local factor was driving me to a school, when he drew my attention to a tall, old woman, who stepped off the narrow road to allow the dogcart to pass. My companion saluted her in Gaelic, to which she responded in a clear, cheery voice. She had evidently been a comely Highland lass in her girlhood. When I asked him who she was, he informed me that she was the last survivor of the MacCodrum family, one of whom was a noted Gaelic bard.

I shall here quote what I once read of this clan. The legend runs that they were metamorphosed into seals. They retained, along with the amphibious shape, the human soul, and at times human form. They were in fact seals by day, but human creatures at night. No MacCodrum for all the world would, if in his proper senses, fire a gun at a seal.

I occasionally stayed a night in the manse of Cromarty. The Rev. Walter Scott, who was then minister, had married a daughter of Dr. Brydon, the famous hero of Kabul, historically referred to as the sole survivor of a British army. As I sat beside her I gathered from her own lips the narrative of her father's miraculous escape. "Poor papa," she said, "was terribly wounded and exhausted before he reached Kabul."

In conclusion, it may not be out of place to mention that when I was a student at Edinburgh University I chanced to see a young man who rose to literary fame. He was lanky, with dark hair and a somewhat sallow complexion. He dropped into the Logic classroom, and, apart from his being an intruder, something about him drew my attention as he seated himself at the door end of the seat directly in front of me. Putting everything together, I am now satisfied that the stranger was Robert Louis Stevenson. He probably came in to pass the time between two classes he may then have been attending.

Chapter XVIII

GAELIC

I f one is to accept the tenor of the old rhyme, a quatrain of which runs:

Music first was heard on earth
In Gaelic accents deep,
When Tubal in his oxter squeezed
The bledder o' a sheep.

Gaelic must indeed be a very ancient language. But setting that aside, one must admit that both from a linguistic and musical point of view it has few equals. When I began examining schools it was spoken much more widely throughout the Highlands than it is now. To meet the disadvantages under which Gaelic-speaking children laboured as far back as 1877, the Code provided that the intelligence of the pupils might be tested by asking them to explain in their native language the meaning of the passages read. If they were able to do so a substantial grant accrued.

Being a native of an eastern county, I was handicapped in my work by knowing no Gaelic. Of necessity, I set myself to study Stewart's *Grammar*. By good luck I had the assistance and guidance of my boon companion, the late Dr. Alexander Macbain, who was at the time rector of Raining's

School in Inverness. He always impressed me with his immense capacity for work, his application, and the thoroughness with which he probed to the bottom of whatever Celtic word or topic he had in hand. His well-known *Etymological Dictionary* I saw growing from week to week. A Gaelic-speaking Inspector, when he saw the volume in manuscript, carefully bound for the author's own private use, knowing its great value to Celtic scholars, exhorted him to have it published. This he ultimately did, though with some reluctance, as candidly I don't think he realised its importance. In point of Celtic scholarship he was undoubtedly one of the most brilliant products of the Highlands.

With the smattering of Gaelic I acquired, I contrived to overtake my work. If I had sympathy with the children who knew little English, the teachers were very tolerant of me who knew less Gaelic. I can recall only one case where the dominie of a denominational school made a base attempt to profit by my lack of knowledge of the language. I had been entrusted with the inspection of his school. Unfortunately the senior pupils taught by himself did not distinguish themselves. Consequently the grant, which the managers could ill spare, suffered. The chief manager and the teacher concocted a letter, which was transmitted to the Department. The gravamen was that I did not make use of Gaelic in my examination of the pupils. The Inspector of the district, an excellent Celtic scholar, alive to the absurdity of such a complaint, in answer to My Lords' demand for an explanation, replied that the pupils attending this particular school were as ignorant of Gaelic as Londoners, otherwise he would not have sent me to inspect it. This was practically true. He knew quite well that they were not being properly taught. Next year I was deputed to examine the same school, as it was considered policy that I should do so. The results were quite in keeping with those of the previous year. Failing to extract anything from the pupils by my use of English, I asked the teacher to test them through the medium of Gaelic. He rather sheepishly replied that he could not speak Gaelic, and that therefore he was unable to comply with my request. Remembering his accusation, I was simply dumfoundered. "If you don't use Gaelic in teaching," said I, "how can you expect me to make use of it in examination?" With that I left him. He was not the type of man to argue with.

By the time the pupils taught by an English-speaking teacher reached the higher standards, I found that they were as a rule able to give an intelligent explanation of the passages they had been reading. Being young, they seemed to be more susceptible of picking up English, which the teacher had to use to the exclusion of Gaelic. I may here mention that one year when at St. Malo I made the acquaintance of the French governess of the German Imperial family. She was the finest speaker of French I ever met. She told me she was not permitted to speak any language save French to her pupils. This brought forcibly to my mind the analogous case of the English-speaking teacher using English only in his work. Still, I am bound to admit that a capable teacher familiar with both Gaelic and English has a decided advantage. Through the medium of the one properly used he can get his pupils to make progress in the other.

Under the Education Authorities, who since 1919 have

the administration in their several counties, more attention than formerly is being given to the teaching of Gaelic. In fact a resurgence is taking place under An Comunn Gaidhealach; but in these days it is uphill work. I have frequently discussed the Gaelic question with Highlanders, who frankly allege that nowadays to get on in the world one must be familiar with the language of the world, which is English, not Gaelic. In the face of such a sentiment, despite every effort to keep alive the flame, it is difficult to see how the hegemony of the Gaelic soul can be preserved.

It is surprising how few persons, who evince a deep interest in Gaelic, know how widely it is spoken and read in Nova Scotia, as well as to a less extent in other provinces of the Canadian Dominion, where natives of the Hebrides have formed agricultural settlements. At least two Established Church clergymen of my acquaintance, both natives of Nova Scotia, came to this country, preached in Gaelic, and got livings — one in Eigg, and the other in Knoydart, in the county of Inverness.

To hear Gaelic spoken to perfection, one has only to be present at the *Ceilidh* (pronounced Kaily) which was a regular feature of Highland life when I first visited the Hebrides. This was a gathering round the glowing peat fire of an evening, when tales of love as well as of witches and warlocks were told. The songs sung at the 'waulking' of the home-spun cloth, handed down through generations, were also repeated. These, mostly in a minor key, would charm the visitor with an ear for music. The tales gained rather than lost by being narrated in the vernacular in awe-inspiring surroundings. To show the nature of them, let me tell in English one of a humorous character connected with the island of Jura, the chief proprietor of which I often met in friendly intercourse. A pawky crofter named McPhail, locally known as Rùsgan, had a peculiar temperament in which wit predominated. The factor of the estate, knowing this, took delight in chaffing him on every favourable opportunity. Long ago it was the custom to give every tenant a glass of whisky when he paid his rent. The factor, who was refreshing himself, said to Rùsgan, who had just deposited his rent, "I think you are far better without a dram, Rùsgan." To this the latter replied in Gaelic, *"An ruð a ni math ðo bhàilliðh Dhiùra, cha dean e cron ð'on Rùsgan McPhail,"* which rendered in English is, "What's good for the Jura factor will do no harm to fleecy McPhail." The multiplicity of newspapers and periodicals scattered all over the islands undoubtedly tends to push the *Ceiliðh* into the background. Education is likewise in no small measure responsible for its gradual disappearance, and most fatal to its continuance will be the introduction of 'wireless,' which less than half a century ago would have been associated with his Satanic Majesty.

More than one teacher that I knew from an eastern county lived long enough in the Highlands to acquire a good colloquial mastery of Gaelic. Some were even able to lead the singing of the Psalms in church, a much more difficult task than conducting a choir in an English-speaking congregation. One lady in Morven in Argyllshire, a native of Clackmannan, learned to read and speak Gaelic fluently. She even put forward pupils who won prizes at competitions open to those proficient in the language of the

Gael. Reference to Morven brings to my mind a unique experience I once had there. This is one of the wildest and most sparsely populated districts of the county. It was in July, 1920, that I happened to be at Lochaline, when I learned that an eyrie containing one eaglet had been accidentally discovered on a cliff overlooking a small loch some miles distant in the interior of a wide stretch of hilly moorland. Accompanied by the young man who made the discovery and the local teacher, I set out to see this object of ever-engrossing interest. After trudging up hill and down dale we halted, and our guide, pointing to an elevation across a heather-clad valley, exclaimed, "It's just on the face of the cliff below that knoll." As we approached the elevation indicated, what struck us was the entire absence of any kind of bird life, and indeed of life of any kind. When we arrived at the top of the cliff our guide, peering over the brink to where the eyrie was situated, exclaimed, "Yes, the eaglet is still there." As several weeks had elapsed since he first made the discovery, it was not surprising to find that it was now fully fledged. To reach the nest the utmost caution had to be exercised. The foothold was precarious, and the least slip would have precipitated one to the foot of the cliff. We moved in single file from ledge to ledge, until only a narrow chasm separated us from the object of our visit. He was truly a beautiful bird, as he cowered in terror in his rough nest of heather on a small ledge overhung with fern-covered rock. What specially impressed me was the lovely golden brown colour of his plumage, and the clean, long, curved claws, sharp as needles. Naturally, he resented our presence, and at once pushed his head into a crevice of the rock behind him. However, on my poking him with my walking-stick, he immediately withdrew it, and, staring at us with fiery-looking eyes, began to utter loud, piercing screams, intended no doubt to summon to his aid the parent birds. This alarmed us, because, though as yet we had seen no sign of these, it was just possible a bolt from the blue might descend to our discomfiture. Luckily, no parent came to the rescue, but I afterwards gathered from a gamekeeper that the two old eagles were no doubt all the time watching us from a great elevation overhead, but, seeing three intruders, they did not venture to attack us. Had I been alone the case might have been different. The eaglet's larder seemed to be more well stocked than varied. There may have been other relics hidden under the bird, but obviously rabbits were its chief food. One lay torn in pieces, another was in a less mangled condition, while a third was practically intact. An unhatched egg lay in the fleshy debris. I should have liked to possess it, but the attempt would have been rather risky. I afterwards learned that this bird found a home in the Scottish Zoo, near Edinburgh. He must have been captured shortly after I saw him, for he seemed then on the verge of soaring aloft to fend for himself. I was glad I had seen the eyrie and embraced an opportunity rarely offered to a member of the inspectorate.

In districts where it was given out that Gaelic was the only language spoken, the Inspector could always have proof of this by listening to the speech of the pupils in the playground. The mixture of English and Gaelic was often amusing. It was wonderful to note how readily the children of strangers, such as Inland Revenue officers, picked up

Gaelic at the school games; nor could one refrain from smiling when he heard Alfred Hoyle speaking Gaelic with a pronounced Cockney accent. Nevertheless, this was inevitable in his new environment. When he grew to manhood he would probably be proud to be taken for a Highlander, fully appreciative of the skirl of the great Highland bagpipe, which he might even have acquired skill in playing.

To get the full flavour of a Gaelic song one has to hear it sung by the Celt on his native heath. I can never forget one warm summer day when I visited Lochbuie school in Mull, that island which Dr. Johnson for some private reason so disliked, but which the poet correctly eulogises thus:

Broad shouldered Mull, the fairest isle that spreads
Its green folds to the sun in Celtic seas.

After concluding their physical drill in the playground, the pupils, arranged in a circle, sang a beautiful Gaelic song. It breathed of subtle inspiration. As the sweet voices of childhood were raised in tuneful melody, which echoed and re-echoed amongst the surrounding heather-clad hills, one could not help realising how much of its stimulating fervour is lost when such a song is sung in a city music hall.

I am afraid comparatively few people, including those of the same persuasion, are aware that the service of the Scottish Episcopal Church is actually conducted in Gaelic in more than one church in the Highlands. To convince a sceptical Roman Catholic priest in Renfrewshire of this I showed him a copy of the prayer-book entirely in Gaelic. It was presented to me by the estimable clergyman of Glencoe.

In the island of Lewis in the latter part of last century there lived more than one individual of the imbecile type. Though of low mentality they were as a rule quite harmless, and were allowed to roam about the townships to which they belonged. As the children were accustomed to see them, it was seldom that they took advantage of their mental defects to harass them in any way. The Lunacy Commissioner, with whom I was well acquainted, saw to it at his periodical visits that they were well looked after, and on the whole they led a not unhappy life. As a fact, amongst their own kith and kin they were viewed and treated with affection. One of these was a man in the parish of Barvas, and as the Commissioner was specially desirous of having a likeness of this particular individual, I contrived to get him to stand before me in the little inn while I sketched him playing one note on an old broken concertina, which was his daily *vade mecum*. Another imbecile was a young woman of pronounced muscular proportions, who, as one passed through her township, took delight in running barelegged after the conveyance in the hope of getting the pennies which thoughtless strangers frequently tossed to her. I say thoughtless, because she was so apt to run till completely exhausted, with the result that she sometimes collapsed in a fit. It was in connection with her that I was once made the victim of a practical joke. One day the district Inspector and I had visited the school in her neighbourhood. Our wagonette was occupied by two ladies, a brother of the

Sheriff, and myself. My seat was in the corner beside the door. As usual the buxom imbecile came running after us, much to the disgust of the refined ladies from Edinburgh, who were not accustomed to the sight in public of one of their own sex clad in nothing save the most necessary apparel. The Inspector, from his seat beside the driver, slewing round, addressed her in Gaelic, with the result that she suddenly mounted the iron step, and, clutching me round the neck, imparted a kiss on my cheek with a sounding smack. So firm was her grip, accentuated by her weight, that she almost pulled me out of the conveyance. It turned out that the Inspector promised her a penny if she would kiss the young man beside the door. She certainly earned it, and went off screaming with laughter, while I sat blushing with feelings hovering between wrath and bewilderment.

I shall conclude this chapter with an amusing episode, in which the Sassenach teacher and the Celtic parson did not see eye to eye in the matter of teaching Gaelic. To a small school in one of the Inner Hebrides a teacher was appointed, whose career had been chiefly in England. He was by nature clever and a good scholar. But, for some reason never satisfactorily explained, his lines had not fallen in pleasant places. He had drifted north, then west, and at last found himself located on this remote island. To the Highland atmosphere, the Celts, and particularly to their language, he never became reconciled. Unfortunately for him, his neighbouring minister was an ardent Celtic scholar, born and bred in the Highlands. It was only natural that he was never tired of proclaiming the merits of his native tongue, with its superabundance of expressive adjectives. Thus it came about that the one regarded himself as the protagonist of English and the other of Gaelic. It was inevitable that the two often came to loggerheads. One evening a public meeting was being held in the schoolroom with a view to enlisting the support of parents for the teaching of Gaelic, as recommended by An Comunn Gaidhealach. The minister took up the matter with commendable zeal. Being the chief speaker, he lauded Gaelic as a spoken language comparable to no other, and strongly advocated its use in school. He had hardly resumed his seat when the teacher, who was sitting not far off, rose to denounce it and everything connected with it. A few young lads seated at the back of the room, more keen to hear a war of words than out of love for their native tongue, at once began to cheer and clap their hands. Turning towards them with an approving smile, the dominie shouted, "That's right, boys; keep it up. I'll take the starch out of his trousers before I am done with him." And, if all accounts be true, he certainly did. Relief came to his Reverence, however, when this 'thorn in his side' betook himself to a region where Gaelic was a foreign language, and his talents could be turned to profitable account in a more populous community. Before leaving, though he did his best to belittle Gaelic, he admitted to a friend that *"Le jeu n'en vaut pas la chandelle."*

Chapter XIX
NÄÄS

I t brought me much joy when manual exercises in the form of Woodwork were introduced into the school curriculum. Rousseau attached much importance to it, and the enlightened Knox, who is recognised as the father of Scottish Education, expressed himself in favour of hand and eye training for the embryonic handicraftsman, for whom the niceties of syntax or the study of logic had no fascination. That the making of wooden articles is from many points of view a valuable discipline cannot be denied.

In the end of last century the certificate for Woodwork issued from the Slöydlärareseminarium of Nääs in Sweden took a premier place. The landowner of the estate on which the seminary is situated selected and adapted certain buildings for instruction in Sloyd, as it was called. While Swedish teachers were preferred as students, others from any nation under the sun were admitted, provided sleeping accommodation for them in that rural district was available. Dr. Salomon, a nephew of the proprietor, whom the late Sir John Struthers of the Scottish Education Department eulogised as a born educationalist, was appointed director. By the way, Sir John himself, when an Inspector of Schools, took a session at Nääs, thus showing the importance he attached to hand and eye training.

It was in 1899 that I determined to secure a certificate

from this world-famous seminary. I was rather late in lodging my application for admission, but by great good luck an American teacher had failed to turn up. I got the bench reserved for her as soon as I arrived from Gottenborg, and immediately plunged *in medias res*, resolved to overtake as many of the models as possible before the end of the session. Being a week late, I found that all the sleeping-rooms were already occupied. However, I was honoured in being relegated to a gorgeous bedroom in the late proprietor's palatial residence about half a mile from the seminary. On the walls were hung beautiful oil paintings by the Montalbas, who, I was told, were nearly related to him. Except for two maidservants I was the sole occupant of the mansion, which, I was told, was originally a royal shooting-box.

That year both male and female teachers from over half the globe were at Nääs, showing that the systematic instruction of pupils in Woodwork was becoming universal. It was a glorious opportunity for one desirous of picking up a foreign language. In one sleeping-place situated in a wood the students were of so many different nationalities that it was known as Babel. With a Rumanian professor nobody could converse, and I was sorry for him.

But while all were instructed in Sloyd, the social side was not neglected. A fellow-student and I hired a boat from a crofter for ten kroner (about ten shillings of our money). We had the sole use of it for eight weeks. Many a pleasant and profitable evening we spent in that boat on the beautiful loch beside the seminary, with Swedish teachers in their native costume for company.

At that time the instruction cost nothing, while a few pounds covered the whole expense of board and lodging. Towards the end of the session I designed and constructed a special model which had to be left behind. No doubt it is still displayed along with many others, including that of Sir John Struthers, on the wall of the exhibition room. Before handing it in I could not help scribbling across it, *'Quod potui perfeci.'*

The session ended, I was honoured by being asked by Dr. Salomon to write a testimonial for the Welshman—a former student—who was instructor for the English-speaking section. It was certainly rather humiliating for the latter that a pupil should be entrusted with such an important task. Still, he was sensible enough to realise that

> *. . . each act is rightest done*
> *Not when it must, but when it may be best.*

I had made up my mind to see more of Sweden before returning home. Accordingly, my companion and I took train for Stockholm, allowed to be the Venice of the North. But the place I was most desirous of visiting was Upsala, the University town. Here lived Linnaeus, the greatest botanist of the eighteenth century. Leaving Stockholm, after a railway journey of sixty-six kilometres, we arrived at our destination, and at once proceeded in the direction of the University. Most visitors first bend their steps to the Cathedral, a huge building in the Gothic style of architecture built of brick. Here are interred Linnaeus and several Swedish kings. The University is most interesting. It dates from 1477. Its library contains more than 200,000 volumes and over 800 manuscripts, many of them being of priceless value. The students wear white-topped caps not unlike those of our own Navy men.

Our first objective was the library, where we were hopeful of seeing the world-famous 'Codex Argenteus,' a manuscript in *Maeso* Gothic, written in gold and silver by Bishop Ulfilas, who translated the Bible into Gothic. It dates from the fourth century. Such a unique treasure was worth coming a long way to see. Unfortunately for us we had arrived on a day when the library was closed. To our dismay we found the great door at the entrance shut. However, in the hope that luck might attend us, I beat long and loudly upon it with my walking-stick. In a little we heard the sound of footsteps. A key was turned, and the door was slowly opened by a pleasant looking, middle-aged gentleman, who proved to be one of the librarians. Not to lose time, and to apprise him of the object of our visit, I pointed to the allusion to the Codex in the guide book which I held in my hand. *"Ja! Ja!* Codex," he said, and at once flung the door wide open. He conducted us to a room in the middle of the floor of which stood a glass case containing the priceless manuscript, open for the scrutiny of all interested in such treasures. Our lack of Swedish prevented us from discussing it with the amiable librarian, who waited patiently till we were satisfied before again closing the shutters. He even permitted my companion, who was armed with a camera, to take a photograph of the volume. It was useless to attempt to thank him in English, so we contented ourselves, and evidently pleased him, by simply saying

"Tack," the Swedish equivalent for 'Thanks,' as he politely bowed us out and shut the door. He knew we were foreigners and had probably come from a far country. Proud of his treasure, and unwilling to disappoint us, with the proverbial Swedish courtesy, for the Swedes are nothing if not polite and obliging, he readily admitted us. I am afraid it is only too true that few librarians in this country would have taken the trouble to act as he did to a couple of inquisitive foreigners.

As we subsequently strolled down an avenue of trees in search of the Arts building we overtook two students with books under their arms. Addressing the nearest one in English, I asked him where this part of the University was situated. He at once replied, very clearly and deliberately. "Come this way. We are going there." His familiarity with English quite surprised me. As we walked along I let him know that I had been a student at Edinburgh University. In this he seemed much interested. He asked no questions, but he evidently understood mine, and had always a slow, correctly-worded reply. When we parted I complimented him on his knowledge of English. He then led me to understand that it was the first time he had ever spoken to an Englishman. I gathered further that at school he had been taught English by a Swede. As I pursued my way to the handsome building which he indicated amongst the trees, I could not help reflecting on the quickness and accuracy with which foreigners do pick up our language, despite its numerous inconsistencies between sound and spelling.

By mid-day we had concluded our visit to the University, and had admired the many things that reminded us of Linnaeus which met us at every turn. Our stomachs next claimed attention, but where to find the needful puzzled us. Upsala is a small town, and restaurants are not too numerous. Going along the principal street, we found out from the number of carts, horses and cattle here, there and everywhere, that it was market day. Farmers, with their wives clad in plain but seemingly comfortable clothes, were stirring about, bargaining and bawling as they do on such occasions in every country. More interested in finding out how these rustics fed than with a view to economy, my companion and I entered a small inn where we saw open apartments on either hand full of natives, male and female, all engaged in a mid-day meal. A stout, active Hebe signed to us to follow her. We found ourselves outside in a sort of annex where were two or three tables covered with cloths spotlessly white. Without any difficulty I got her to understand that we wanted '*middag*,' which is Swedish for dinner. With a frank *"Ja! ja!"* she proceeded to set on the table two bottles of lager beer, as we concluded, by way of appetiser. Following upon this came five or six courses of plain but excellently cooked food, for the whole of which she asked with her *politest "Var sa god"* (if you please) one kroner, about equal to one shilling for the two of us. For quantity and quality I am bound to admit that it was the cheapest lunch I ever got in all my travels either at home or abroad. There was absolutely no attempt to take advantage of the stranger within the gates. We evidently paid the same price as the peasants. But it is more than likely that even then the price would have been a very different one had we lunched in the Stadshotellet or city hotel. And yet at that date Sweden was probably the cheapest country in Europe in which to travel. Since the Great War I have heard that things are greatly changed, and that even a session at Nääs is now expensive.

On returning to my own sphere of labour armed with the Nääs diploma, I felt myself in the position of being able to offer advice which the manual instructors, cognisant of my qualifications, were not slow to appreciate.

Chapter XX

IONA AND HINBA

ssociated as I have recently been officially for more than thirteen years with Argyll, I may be excused for writing some succinct details regarding two islands which, though small in area, are of supreme ecclesiastical importance. These I gleaned from reliable materials in my possession. The islands referred to are Iona and Hinba, the former being the only one of the two now inhabited. In the first place let me deal with it.

"Put off thy shoes from off thy feet, for the place whereon thou standest is holy ground," was the text that rose to my mind when I first set foot on this world-renowned shrine of medieval devotion, at Baile Mor, the only village on the island. *Ioua* was the name by which it was known in the oldest manuscripts. In far-off centuries it was simply called Hy or Yi, meaning island, also Icolmkill; that is, island of Columba of the church. Though ecclesiastically renowned, it is a comparatively small Hebridean island, being about three miles long and a mile to a mile and a half wide. Its highest point is *Dunii*, which is only 330 feet above sea level. Nowadays with Iona is associated Staffa, with its huge cave, lying to the northwards. By the late Professor Blackie these islands are thus beautifully referred to:

"Staffa is for everybody who has eyes: Iona for the few

who have knowledge. Staffa requires only one idea to make
it sublime, vizt., God. Iona, to excite any sensation at all
beyond the vague sentiment that hangs round an old ruin,
demands in the spectator a hall of memory richly hung with
the pictures of early European civilization."

In 563 A.D. Columba, the founder of the Scots Celtic
Church, with twelve followers, including the saintly Oran,
who declared he could make out Ireland from sacred
Oronsay, set sail for Iona. Columba had taken a vow, as
tradition has it, that he would not settle on any island from
which Ireland could be seen. They landed from a light hide-
covered *curach* at a small bay called Port-a-churraich, where
I once picked up a number of beautiful green pebbles.

As is well known, Columba was born at Gartan in
Donegal in 521 A.D., his father being one of the eight sons
of O' Neil of the nine hostages, supreme monarch of all
Ireland. His mother was a daughter of the royal house of
Leinster. His proper name was Corinthian, but his companions called him Columan or Dove. From Adamnan, sixth
abbot of Iona, his biographer, we get much information
regarding him and the saintly life he led. A good deal of it,
however, must be traditional, but it is nevertheless valuable.

After being ordained priest he entered upon his labours
with apostolic zeal, and when only twenty-five years of age
(546 A.D.) he founded a monastery in Derry, and six or
seven years later another in Durrow. We gather that about
this time he embroiled himself in the civil strifes of his countrymen, and that, as a result of his instigating the battle of
Cooldrevny he was excommunicated by an Irish
Ecclesiastical Synod in 561 A.D. However, the justice of the

sentence was challenged by some high ecclesiastics. At the same time there is no doubt that this had much to do with his leaving Ireland and betaking himself to Scotland.

His close Irish connection with the nobility, combined with his great piety, gave him extensive influence wherever he went. He is said to have been a man of great personal beauty. His height, his voice, as well as his cordiality, were remarkable.

He got a grant of Iona from Conall, son of Comghall, king of the Scots. Here he erected his cloister. It was exceedingly primitive, the walls being of wattles. There are no trees in Iona, and it is more than probable that there were none in Columba's time, so he and his followers had just to use the material they found most suitable and convenient for their purpose.

The conversion of the Pictish nation to the faith of Christ was his first great achievement. The scholarly Dr. Norman MacLeod in his Gaelic life of St. Columba, after referring to the great difficulties the saint encountered amongst the Druids and their uncivilised Caledonian followers, tells how Scotland was at that time like a vast wilderness, without roads of any kind. Through the thick, dark pine woods wild beasts roamed everywhere. The fierce Picts were then the inhabitants of the Western Isles, Western Highlands, and the Orkneys. The Roman influence seemed never to have penetrated thus far during all the centuries of their rule in Great Britain.

For thirty-four years Columba worked hard founding churches and spreading the gospel of Christ, thus effectively condemning the Druidic teaching. His monastery in Iona was regarded as the Mother Church, and as such was venerated by the Scots in Britain and Ireland, as well as by the Angles of the North of England. From this centre his emissaries were sent out to nearly all the counties of Scotland, where we find places deriving their names from these holy men. Monasteries and abbeys sprang up everywhere. The order of St. Columba was one of the most extensive. In Iona the saint in due course received the homage of mitred bishops and crowned monarchs. Kings are said to have sought his advice. In his presence mutual friendship and goodwill were entered on and sealed by oath on three stones, known as the *Three black stones of Iona*, supposed to correspond to the Trinity. As to what became of these history is silent.

But, though kings consulted him, and he possessed more than regal power, the house he occupied was but a hut made of planks. He slept upon a hard floor with a stone for a pillow. To this lowly abode he repaired after his daily toil with the monks was at an end. It is recorded that he rode about the island on a favourite white horse. In his hut he spent much time transcribing the sacred text of Scripture. The Venerable Bede in his *Historia Ecclesiastica Gentis Anglorum* tells us that waxed tablets for writing were used by the disciples of Columba in Iona at the close of the seventh century. A very touching reference to the saint's death is recorded. When he reached the 33rd Psalm he stopped and said, "Baithean will write the rest." This St. Baithean was steward of Iona, and succeeded Columba as abbot. A clachan in Strathglass in Inverness-shire is dedicated to this saint. But that by the way. On the following morning Columba hastened before the monks, and, kneeling in front of the high altar, died in the arms of Diarmid, blessing all his disciples. This was on the ninth day of June, 597 A.D.

For centuries after his death Iona was the most venerated sanctuary of the Celts. It was the nursery of bishops, the centre of learning and religious knowledge. Seventy kings or princes were said to have been brought there and buried at the feet of the saint. The Celtic poet Evan MacColl in one of his plaintive odes to Iona wrote:

Sacred Isle of Iona
Where saints and heroes
Live in stone.

Till the end of the eighth century Iona was scarcely second to any monastery in the British Isles. But, as happened to Rome, a day came when misfortune overtook it. In 795 A.D. the fierce heathen Norsemen landed and burned the sacred edifice, and again in 802 A.D. In 806 A.D. it is said sixty-eight persons were massacred. A second slaughter followed in 825 A.D. Then in 986 A.D. ruthless Norsemen slew the abbot and fifteen of his monks. Thus tragedy followed tragedy. Tradition maintains that the bones of Columba were removed for safety to Kells in Ireland and Dunkeld in Scotland. Later, the monastery was repaired by Margaret, Queen of Malcolm Canmore. It is said that Magnus, King of Norway, in his predatory expedition of 1098 A.D., recoiled with awe when he essayed to enter the rebuilt sacred edifice.

The crosses in Iona are world famous. But few who rave about them seem to be aware of the exquisite crosses at Kildalton in Islay. One still standing outside the broken-down walls of the ruined church is a close rival to any of those in Iona. I never visited the small school of Kintour in this neighbourhood without having another look at it and other crosses within about two hundred yards of the public road. I believe, however, their existence is well known in Ireland, which can be seen from this point.

No building now remains in Iona which can claim to have sheltered St. Columba or his disciples. Ruins there are to-day in great number. The present cathedral, now reroofed and completed as a place of worship, was probably built in the early part of the thirteenth century. For centuries everything was allowed to go to wreck and ruin, but the sacred memories and traditions associated with the island were never permitted to pass into oblivion. It is the sacred associations connected with the saint's name and mission that draw travellers from all quarters of the globe to Iona.

But let us glance at the island as it is to-day. Some of the inhabitants, who seldom leave the island, are not too well off. They are glad when the tourist season commences. The school would be very small but for the number of pauper children boarded out by the parochial authorities about Glasgow. These are very well looked after, and the remuneration derived from their residence there is a welcome addition to the precarious living of the natives. Some years ago a controversy arose as to the propriety of introducing these children to the Sacred Isle, seeing that they came from the city slums, where some of them had been associating with the lowest types of humanity, and were even their offspring. Personally, at my visits to the island I saw no trace of evil contamination, nor did I hear of any. The children were well fed, bright and betrayed the usual quickness of intelligence often characteristic of those unfortunates accustomed to poverty and hardknocks.

A writer on Highland subjects has remarked that questionable heredity can be overcome by healthy surroundings and good training; in other words, that the offspring of criminals, if rescued from vicious environment, may become respectable citizens. With these sentiments, from what I have seen, I quite agree. So much for Iona.

And now let me make some remarks about the other island, supremely sacred, also associated with St. Columba, namely, Hinba. Probably not one in a thousand ever heard of this island. Yet it actually contains ruins which bring us face to face with the great saint. Almost due west of the island of Luing lie the Gravelloch Group or Isles of the Sea, one of which is Hinba, the most southerly of this uninhabited group. It is locally known as Eilach na Naoimh; that is, 'The graveyard of the saints.' One or two antiquaries erroneously made it Eilan Naoimh or 'Holy Island.' It is only little more than a mile long, with high cliffs on its northwest side. The slope is to the south-east. The soil is fertile, and the grazing for sheep excellent. The most convenient way of reaching it is by motor boat from Easdale on the mainland. The journey takes fully an hour. The landing is made at a small creek beset with rocks.

The ecclesiastical history of Hinba takes one back to

542 A.D., when St. Bride and St. Brendan laid its foundation. There is no doubt that St. Columba made this lone spot his *Diseart* or retreat from the exacting cares of Iona. One can easily picture him standing on St. Brendan's hill, 270 feet above the sea level, looking south-westward towards Ireland and recalling the pomp and splendour he used to enjoy there in the early days of his youth.

Close to the landing-place is a well scooped out of the solid rock, with water running pure as it has done for centuries. A little farther on is a small green plateau covered with ruins that, as has been well said, have no parallel in the country. They are far older than any on Iona, or even on Oronsay, off the south coast of Colonsay. Here is the chapel with walls intact. It is twenty-two feet long, eleven feet wide, with walls three feet thick and nearly nine feet high. The doorway even is still complete, and a small double splayed window faces the east. Heather now grows on the top of the walls. Near the chapel are traces of what must have been the monastery itself. Farther on is the burying-ground. Only by probing the soil can any trace of stones be detected. There is, however, one tombstone with a rude Celtic cross on it, which points to a remote antiquity. Outside this burying-ground is perhaps the oldest gravestone on the island. On it is inscribed a very primitive cross. Remains of what had once been well built houses are fairly plentiful, but throughout there is an entire absence of lime or any kind of mortar used in their construction. The walls are made up of thick slabs of slate laid horizontally above one another. In the Isles of the Sea, and Easdale on the mainland, slate is plentiful. Till recent years the quarries at the latter place did a large trade in roofing slates. All the houses on Hinba were small, with very narrow windows. Perhaps lighting was sacrificed to warmth. The small dwellings near the chapel had evidently been used as a domestic part of the monastery. A curious little building with one end square and the other round attracts attention. At the semi-circular end there is a hole in the wall which leads downwards probably to the furnace, which thus formed the kiln on which the monks dried their grain before hand grinding it. Southwards from the chapel is an underground cell. It looks as if from it the chief supply of water had been obtained. One can descend through a passage lined with flagstones and having large slabs overhead. At the bottom is a chamber about five feet in diameter. Behind this there was an irregular recess. There is a tradition that erring monks did penance here, sitting with hands wedged between the slabs of the recess.

In a mound of earth about 150 yards from the chapel it is believed that Aethne, the mother of St. Columba, was buried. Here is a small cairn with two upright stones, on one of which is a small Greek cross with no trace of an inscription.

The two monks' cells claim special attention. They are not unlike diminutive rounded stacks seen at glass-works, or old-fashioned straw beehives. The larger one was eighteen feet in height and fifteen in diameter, with a very low connecting door between them. And be it noted that, although there are traces of houses of more recent date, almost all the ruins on Hinba are ecclesiastical. Here vandalism got no footing during all the centuries. Iona, on the other hand, as I have already related, fared differently. Not a fragment of its once fine altar piece now remains. In all probability stones with the most sacred associations were used in the construction of ordinary dwelling-houses. Adamnan records incidents which go to prove that St. Columba frequently visited Hinba for the purpose already mentioned. There was doubtless a monastery here before the saint set foot on Iona. Nor should this fact be over-looked. The Columban erections on Iona, being either turf huts or wattled buildings, have ages ago disappeared. On the other hand, on Hinba are still to be seen the imperish-able slabs, which lent themselves so readily for building purposes. Thus in many respects this lonely uninhabited Isle of the Sea even exceeds Iona in ecclesiastical interest.

When the slate quarries at Easdale were at the height of their prosperity there was a considerable population in that neighbourhood. But since the work proved unprof-itable the quarries have been closed, and a school built for two hundred or more pupils is now occupied by a few children taught by a single teacher. As a pious old clergyman said when I was discussing the sad change which had taken place, *"Bidh gach ni mar is àill le Dia"*, anglice, 'All will be as God wills.'

Chapter XXI

THEN AND NOW

T ruly many are the changes connected with education that time has wrought. Up to the middle of last century, and for years after, the school was a very unpretentious building. Often in country districts, except for the unusual number of windows, it could hardly be distinguished from an ordinary farmhouse. When the teacher's dwelling was not above the schoolroom, it consisted of one storey with a low ceiling without ventilators of any kind. The windows were small, with tiny oblong-shaped panes. Long, broad wooden desks were attached to the walls. Facing these the pupils sat on deal forms without backs. In the desks there were no holes for ink-wells. The pupils brought fuel for the fires. How it was obtained was never questioned. On their arrival in the morning it was tossed into a corner ready for use when required.

Each pupil carried his own supply of ink to school. In my mind's eye I see the teacher sharpening the quills with which I first essayed to learn penmanship; also the boy distributing from a receptacle, not unlike a maid's modern knife box, the headlines engraved in copperplate on long strips of cardboard. I hear the pupil who had finished with one shouting, "I'll thank you for a headline." The introduction of steel pens by reason of the following incident is deeply impressed on my memory. When I asked my father for a penny to buy one he turned on me and, curling his brows, exclaimed, "How can you write with a piece of iron?" But the piece of iron had come to stay, and the substitution of the steel pen for the quill was encouraged by the teacher, who welcomed any innovation which would relieve him of the daily, irksome task of quill sharpening. The quill, however, is not yet obsolete. Bunches of excellent quality are no doubt still supplied from His Majesty's Stationery Office. As I had no particular fancy for them, I am afraid I was not slow to comply with my father's request for an occasional specimen.

In those days education was not compulsory. Had all the children in a parish come forward the local school would have been filled to overflowing. I can remember seeing farm servants, big, bearded men, seated in the back desks, which creaked under their weight. They had felt the disadvantage under which the laboured in not being able to read, write, and count; so they gave up manual labour for what they called a *raith* at school. This constituted a period of three months in the winter time when outdoor work was practically at a standstill. All paid fees. These were a very important part of the teachers emoluments.

Half a century ago lads whose aspirations soared beyond hard manual toil were not awanting. When I was attending the Grammar School in Old Aberdeen, taught by Dr. William Dey, a brother of the Inspector of Schools, I knew young men of twenty who every morning entered the classroom in a state of perspiration. They were come of poor parents who could not afford to pay for the education of their sons. But the lads themselves were pushful, and deter-mined to rise in the world. Accordingly, they rose with the lark, and earned money by labouring in local granite quarries for some hours every morning before hastening to studies in the Grammar School. Oatmeal, butter, eggs, and the inevitable bag of potatoes were their chief sustenance. On such food some of them became brilliant classical scholars. This, however, is a tale of the past, at which the pampered young student of to-day is apt to smile with incredulity.

The 'lad o' pairts' was always in the favour of his teacher, who, if he happened to be a University graduate, was only too pleased to find a pupil smart enough to be pushed on in Classics or Mathematics. To him he devoted no end of attention, often to the neglect of less promising ones. The result was that he proceeded direct from the parish school to the University with a bursary earned by competition.

In charge of parish schools were many able men, who in the north-eastern counties were not infrequently licenti-ates of the Church of Scotland. They held office *ad vitam aut culpam*, or as an Act of 1803 has it, 'because the labours of this most useful body of men have been of essential impor-tance to the public welfare.' Regarding this type of teacher a humorous writer has aptly remarked, "The parochial dominie has left behind him a record of service inseparably connected with the national characteristics which have given Scotland her unique position among the nations; in acknowledgement of which success successive generations have magnanimously rewarded him with the maximum of mouth honour and the minimum of oatmeal."

As time went on things were changed. Education assumed a new phase. With the passing of the Act of 1872 every child had to be educated. Then arose the question of school accommodation. Hitherto a few schools in existence belonged either to the Established or Free Church, with Government Inspectors appointed under each denomination. But another kind of school of the most humble pretensions in which the seeds of learning were frequently sown was the 'dame's' school. It was common in rural districts, and was as a rule taught by an oldish woman as a means of livelihood. To the alphabet, with some very elementary Reading, Writing and Arithmetic, she devoted her sole attention. The pupils supplied her with suitable straws, called 'windle straes,' for pointing to the letters as they pronounced them. It is interesting to note that the foundation of Hugh Miller's education was laid in a dame's school.

I have before me the description of a typical dame's school given in the 'blue book' of 1841 by Her Majesty's Inspector of Schools, when education was then under the Committee of Council on Education. Let me quote it:

"In one of the dame's schools I found 30 children from 2 to 7 years of age. The room was a cellar about 10 feet square and about 7 feet high. The only window was less than 18 inches square, and not made to open. Although it was a warm day, a fire was burning, and the door, through which alone any air could be admitted, was shut. Of course then the room was close and hot; but there was no remedy. The damp subterraneous walls required, as the old woman assured us, a fire throughout the year. If she opened the door the children would rush out to light and liberty, while the cold blast rushing in would torment her aged bones with rheumatism. Still further to restrain their vagrant propensities, and to save them from the danger of tumbling into the fire, she crammed the children as closely as possible in a dark corner at the foot of her bed. Here they sat in the pestiferous obscurity, totally destitute of books, and without light enough to enable them to read had books been placed in their hands. Six children indeed out of 30 had brought some two-penny books; but these also, having been made to circulate through 60 little hands, were now so well soiled and tattered as to be rather the memorials of past achievements than the means of leading the children to fresh exertion. The only remaining instruments of instruction possessed by the dame were a glassful of sugar plums near the tattered leaves on the table in the centre of the room, and a cane by its side; every point in instruction being thus secured by the good old rule of mingling the useful with the sweet." On this state of matters I leave my readers to comment.

When the Act of 1872 was enforced schools of this type became unnecessary and ceased to exist. To meet the new situation, schools pretty much as we see them to-day sprang up like mushrooms all over the country. The Act made Reading, Writing and Arithmetic only compulsory. Gradually other branches, for which grants were paid, found a place in the curriculum.

One of the worst features of the Education Act was its assumption that all children, or at least a majority of them, were of equal intellectual ability. The grant to a school depended in large measure on the 'pass,' the term applied to the summarised results. Accordingly, it was only to be expected that the teacher, particularly if he was paid a share of the grant, would endeavour by hook or crook, the synonym for corporal punishment and bullying, to cram into his pupils sufficient to ensure that the exactions of Her Majesty's emissary would be met. The ability of the teacher generally determined the pressure he put on his pupils. Many a poor child that would to-day be in a mentally defective school must have suffered terribly in the years when his life should have been sunniest. As a boy I knew a parochial teacher who almost daily at the Bible lesson inflicted corporal punishment on a poor imbecile boy, the son of a labouring man, because of his inability to commit to memory the answers to the questions in the Shorter Catechism. I see his pitiful face and hear his cries at this moment. Nor should I be surprised if, when he grew to manhood, he eschewed everything savouring of religion and never darkened a church door.

While I am on the subject of punishment I cannot help recording that the favourite punishment inflicted by a dominie of the old school in a district of the Highlands which I used to visit was the administration of castor oil. He did this through no anxiety for the physical welfare of his pupils. It was simply intended as a punishment because the child nauseated it. Ultimately, as might be expected, he found himself in a police court and was duly fined.

While the education of every child was insisted on, the qualification of the teachers was not overlooked. The pupil-teacher system was soon in full swing. Whatever may have been its failings, it must be admitted that it served its purpose. Many a teacher of distinction completed an apprenticeship, and, if his scholarship was not of a very advanced character, the daily practice he had in teaching well what he did know was no small compensation. In due course encouragement was given to Normal School students to attend classes at the University, where an increasing number finished by taking the M.A. degree.

A few old teachers in remote parts, who had hitherto been non-certificated, came forward to the annual examination for certificates. A sorry appearance some of them made, but the ambition to rise in the profession was laudable. I heard of one who, in answer to a question on School Management bearing on the construction of a time-table, wrote across the space, "I would give a whilie to everything." No doubt he did, and who dare say that after all he did not teach well and was in all likelihood

A man to all his country dear,
And passing rich with forty pounds a year!

As time wore on drastic changes in the educational system took place. Payment by results was gradually abolished. The pupils were to be examined collectively, not individually. The election of School Boards every three years also came to an end, and not a day too soon. Under the School Board the teacher who was unpopular led a miserable life. Even the persecution by one unscrupulous member might end in his dismissal. Further, I have known of more than one case where the teacher's being an adherent of a particular church was not to his advantage.

A sweeping change took place in 1919 when the last Act took effect. By it the administration of education in a county is entrusted to an elected body called the Education Authority. To-day, however, a Government Rating Bill is before Parliament, which aims at reducing the number of administrative bodies, and substituting a system of unified control, financial as well as administrative, with a view to greater efficiency and economy. This, it is claimed, would obviate overlapping and redundancy of public services. Under the Bill education would be entrusted to a Committee of the Town or County Council as the case might be. At present opinions are divided as to whether or not this would be a retrograde step. Should the Bill become law time will show. Meantime it is gratifying to note that whatever changes have hitherto been effected in educational administration the efficiency of the schools has been gradually improved, and the industrious teacher can now do his work without harassment and the petty jealousies that tend to make life intolerable. Years have passed since his salary was in large measure dependent upon the 'pass' of his school. In those days teaching was one of the poorly-paid professions. Now it is one of the best, and justly so, for education is the backbone of a nation, and, as has been well said, 'the labourer is worthy of his hire.'

One would be inclined to think that the training of teachers, particularly in its academic aspect, is now nearly as perfect as it can be. The desirability of a University degree is a step in the right direction, while a thorough grounding in the theory of education ought to secure efficiency in the practice.

As illustrating the progress in comparatively recent years, it may be mentioned that there are special classes and schools for children of low mentality. In these they are graded and taught with the maximum of care and the minimum of pressure.

Incredible as it may appear, children who are both deaf and dumb are also taught in special schools to articulate words and perform ordinary school exercises of various kinds with wonderful proficiency. Naturally, the teachers have to be both patient and painstaking. Their task is often so arduous and heart-breaking that one wonders how they have the courage to persist in it. The ingenious methods they adopt merit the greatest admiration. No class of teachers deserves more credit for the marvellous results they achieve.

Nor has the education of blind children been over-looked. For these throughout the country there are special schools and classes, where they are instructed in ordinary subjects, including manual exercises tending to develop concentration and intellectual application. Their progress is often remarkable. Some pursue the study of advanced subjects; and in recent years there have been one or two cases of blind students obtaining a degree—and even an honours degree—at Edinburgh University.

The progress of education in Scotland has been well described as a record of extraordinary self-denial, perseverance and idealism on the part of both teachers and pupils. As a result Scotsmen fill many of the most prominent positions in all parts of the globe where English is the spoken language.

May the years to come provide a record of achievements no less worthy.

Some other publications by Acair:

FOOTFALL IN LEWIS *by Robert M Adam*

ST KILDAN HERITAGE *by Calum Ferguson*

THE LIVING PAST *by Donald MacLeod*

MUIR IS TÌR *by George MacLeod*

LORD OF THE ISLES *by Nigel Nicolson*

THE ISLANDERS AND THE ORB
THE HISTORY OF THE
HARRIS TWEED INDUSTRY 1835-1995
by Janet Hunter

THE BOOK OF BARRA
by Dr John Lorne Campbell & Compton MacKenzie

WEST OVER SEA *by D A Pochin Mould*

THREE DARK DAYS *by Kenneth MacDonald*

A SHILLING FOR YOUR SCOWL
by James Shaw Grant

MORRISON OF THE BOUNTY
by James Shaw Grant